TIME
The Year in Review
2008

Change from the ground up *John McCain's surprise choice for running mate, Alaska governor Sarah Palin, became the first woman to run on the Republican Party ticket for national office*

TIME

MANAGING EDITOR Richard Stengel
DEPUTY MANAGING EDITOR Adi Ignatius
ART DIRECTOR Arthur Hochstein

The Year in Review 2008

EDITOR Kelly Knauer
DESIGNER Ellen Fanning
PICTURE EDITOR Patricia Cadley
WRITER/RESEARCHER Matthew McCann Fenton
COPY EDITOR Bruce Christopher Carr

TIME INC. HOME ENTERTAINMENT
PUBLISHER Richard Fraiman
GENERAL MANAGER Steven Sandonato
EXECUTIVE DIRECTOR, MARKETING SERVICES Carol Pittard
DIRECTOR, RETAIL & SPECIAL SALES Tom Mifsud
DIRECTOR, NEW PRODUCT DEVELOPMENT Peter Harper
ASSISTANT DIRECTOR, NEWSSTAND MARKETING Laura Adam
ASSISTANT DIRECTOR, BRAND MARKETING Joy Butts
ASSOCIATE COUNSEL Helen Wan
SENIOR BRAND MANAGER, TWRS/M Holly Oakes
BOOK PRODUCTION MANAGER Suzanne Janso
DESIGN AND PREPRESS MANAGER Anne-Michelle Gallero
ASSOCIATE BRAND MANAGER Michela Wilde
ASSISTANT PREPRESS MANAGER Alex Voznesenskiy

SPECIAL THANKS

Glenn Buonocore, Susan Chodakiewicz, Margaret Hess,
Brynn Joyce, Robert Marasco, Brooke Reger, Mary Sarro-Waite,
Ilene Schreider, Adriana Tierno

EZRA SHAW—GETTY IMAGES

ISBN 10: 1-60320-047-9 • ISBN 13: 978-1-60320-047-9 • ISSN: 1097-5721
TIME Books is a trademark of Time Inc.

We welcome your comments and suggestions about TIME Books. Please write to us
at: TIME Books; Attention: Book Editors; PO Box 11016; Des Moines, IA 50336-1016

If you would like to order any of our hardcover Collector's Edition books, please
call us at 1-800-327-6388 (Monday through Friday, 7 a.m.–8 p.m., or Saturday, 7
a.m.–6 p.m., Central time).

COVER PICTURE CREDITS:
FRONT COVER: Obamas: Pablo Martinez Monsivais—AP Images; McCain/Palin:
Ron Edmonds—AP Images; sign: Rich Pedroncelli—AP Images; Olympics
fireworks: Gamma—Eyedea—Zuma Press; The Joker: ©Warner Brothers
Entertainment Inc.; Phelps: Phil Walter—Getty Images; Clinton: Robyn Beck—
AFP—Getty Images; Newman: Douglas Kirkland—Corbis
BACK COVER: Woods/Mediate: Doug Pensinger—Getty Images; Stockbroker:
Richard Drew—AP Images; Russert: Jocelyn Augustino—Redux; Mormon
woman: Tony Gutierrez—AP Images; Dalai Lama: James Nachtwey—VII;
Galveston Island: David J. Phillip—AP Images

PRINTED IN THE UNITED STATES OF AMERICA

Drowning *Swimmer Michael Phelps greets his family after the U.S. squad won the 4 x 100-m medley relay at the Beijing Olympics on Aug. 17*

Contents

Blue skies *Democratic presidential candidate Barack Obama demonstrates his appeal by drawing a crowd of 100,000 to the Gateway Arch in St. Louis on Oct. 18. Sixteen days later, Obama convincingly defeated Republican John McCain to win the election*

The dark mood grew darker as the months ticked by and the credit crunch driving the U.S. economy's slow-motion topple accelerated it into a full-blown crash

Images

Wall Street, New York City, Oct. 10

The Reckoning

When veteran TIME photographer Anthony Suau snapped a man on Wall Street throwing his hands to the heavens in dismay as stock prices melted down, he captured not just the mood of a moment but all the anxiety of a dispirited year in America. Signs of trouble were everywhere, from the FOR SALE: FORECLOSURE notices on the lawns of suburban McMansions to the polls that showed only 9% of Americans believed their nation was on the right course. In a national election year, the candidates of both major parties ran as agents of change, with Democrat Barack Obama branding Republican John McCain as a clone of unpopular President George W. Bush, while McCain strenuously sought to distance himself from a lame-duck President whose approval ratings were among the lowest ever recorded— though higher than those of the Democratic-majority Congress. The dark mood grew darker as the months ticked by and the credit crunch driving the U.S. economy's slow-motion topple accelerated it into a full-blown crash: firms that had seemed sturdy pillars of the nation's wealth were exposed as hollow shells, and trillions of dollars of Americans' wealth went up in smoke in a stock-market meltdown. Diagnosis: "The public's trust has vanished," according to TIME's Michael Grunwald. Treatment: to be determined.

CHRISTOPHER MORRIS—VII FOR TIME

Up Close and Personal

At his best as a speaker when he abandoned a podium to connect directly with voters, Senator John McCain made extensive use of the town-hall format in 2008, as he succeeded in resurrecting his campaign—widely regarded as over in the summer of 2007—to win the Republican Party's presidential nomination. McCain held more than 100 town-hall events in New Hampshire alone, where he defeated rival Mitt Romney to reignite his chances. In June, he challenged presumptive Democratic nominee Senator Barack Obama to hold a series of weekly town-hall meetings during the campaign, but Obama's campaign rejected the offer. Above, McCain, then 71, speaks during the Florida GOP primary. Two boys snagged upfront perches at this event, but reporters often noted that McCain's crowds were all of a piece: the majority of attendees were older, white voters.

Rock Star

Senator Barack Obama greets enthusiastic supporters at the University of Maryland. In contrast to McCain, Obama, 46 in this picture, attracted throngs of young, ethnically diverse voters to his events, and his early campaign was bolstered by a YouTube music video in which young musicians and movie stars endorsed him. An inspiring orator who exuded charisma, Obama was often attacked as offering a politics long on style and short on substance, first by his rivals for the Democratic nomination and later by the GOP in the general election. When the McCain campaign hammered at Obama's lack of experience as a critical distinction between the two men, polls showed voters were receptive to the charge. But when McCain chose a newcomer to national politics, Alaska Governor Sarah Palin, as his running mate, he was forced to drop that line of attack.

Baghdad, Iraq, Jan. 18

Head Games

For years U.S. soldiers in occupied Iraq fought frustration, cultural conflicts, suicide bombings and sectarian insurgencies. In 2008 they finally got a chance to take a deep breath and even indulge in a little horseplay with locals. Thanks to the general success of the surge strategy that sent 30,000 additional American troops to the occupied land beginning in January 2007 and the roll-out of new tactics to deal with Iraq's welter of competing factions, Iraqi-on-Iraqi violence dropped sharply, and American fatalities decreased from 126 in May, 2007, to 23 in December of that year.

Here, U.S. Army Captain Joel Brown, left, and an unidentified soldier, right, receive head scarves from the commander of a branch of Concerned Local Citizens, a U.S.-supported civil security group, in Baghdad's Mekanik neighborhood. In establishing such local groups and paying monthly stipends to their members—many of them former insurgents—U.S. and Iraqi strategists hoped to offer Iraqis a stake in their own protection and build a network of Iraqi-staffed security forces that eventually could be integrated into the national police force.

GLEB GARANICH—REUTERS—LANDOV

Gori, Georgia, Aug. 9

Agony in Georgia

The short, brutal war between Georgia and Russia in August left Georgia's military battered and its countryside scorched by bombs and tank fire. The fighting, which officially ended Aug. 12, when Moscow agreed to a cease-fire, left some 1,000 dead and injured and forced tens of thousands of Georgians and ethnic Russians living in and around Georgia's breakaway region of South Ossetia to flee their homes. Gori, a Georgian town close to the border with South Ossetia, was hit hard: at left, a Georgian man cradles the body of a relative killed by Russian bombs.

Awash with profits from natural resources, Russia has become a new economic power. The invasion of Georgia showed that Prime Minister Vladimir Putin, who continues to run Russia through his handpicked successor as President, Dmitri Medvedev, is ready to reassert his nation's primacy in its neighborhood and is prepared to stand up to both the U.S. and the European Union.

Mianzhu City, China, May 25

Shame!

It might be a scene from the bad old days of China's Cultural Revolution of the 1960s: a party official weathering public humiliation by a group of outraged citizens. But this encounter took place in China's Sichuan province, weeks after the nation's most devastating earthquake since 1976 killed some 70,000 people and left millions homeless. Schools were particularly hard hit by the natural disaster. Many of them—built quickly and on the cheap as officials were bribed to look away—collapsed all too easily, killing thousands of children. At left, local Communist Party leader Jiang Guohua is berated by parents marching in protest and bearing pictures of their children, as he pleads with them not to take their concerns to national authorities.

A surprisingly candid Lin Qiang, vice inspector of the Sichuan provincial education department, told the Chinese news service Xinhua, "If we educational officials hadn't left loopholes for corruption, the collapsed buildings could have been as solid [as those that remained standing]." He added that "seeking truth is more important than losing face."

San Angelo, Texas, April 14, 2008

Stranger in a Strange Land

Texas state authorities raided the Yearning for Zion Ranch of the Fundamentalist Church of Latter Day Saints (FLDS) on April 3 and took more than 400 children into custody. Many of the children's mothers followed them, igniting a clash of cultures that produced such dramatic images as the one at right. Yet members of the sect don't shun every aspect of modernity. As TIME's Hilary Hylton reported, at the 2007 trial of FLDS leader Warren Jeffs: "Young women dressed in the FLDS prim, prairie-style fashions testified … that they listened to 'Uncle Warren's' teachings on their iPods." After the '08 raid, FLDS mothers created websites to plead their cause.

In the FLDS world, young mothers are proud symbols of a central tenet of the faith: only "celestial marriage" [polygamy] gains believers admission to the highest level of Heaven. When FLDS girls reach puberty, they are required to marry, usually into the existing families of older men. As Bruce Perry, a Texas psychiatrist who is an authority on such groups, noted to Hylton: "The state is not saying 'Don't wear those dresses.' It's saying you cannot have sex with 12-year-olds."

Liverpool, U.K., July 18

Windjammers

The past and potential future of energy mingled in Britain in July, when some 100 restored sailing ships arrived in Liverpool for a Tall Ships regatta. As they entered the harbor, the vessels passed through the Burbo Bank windfarm, which was completed in 2007 as part of a major investment in alternative energy initiated by the U.K.'s Labour government. The program aims to build thousands of new wind turbines in the next decades; the Burbo Bank farm has 25 of the big spinners.

The figure in the foreground breaking the waves is not a human; it is a statue by British sculptor Antony Gormley, part of his *Another Place* series, in which 100 cast-iron body forms were rooted along 3 km (1.8 miles) of Liverpool's Crosby Beach. The large work had previously been installed on beaches in Germany, Norway and Belgium; its figures are alternately obscured and exposed by the flow of the tides.

Touché!

Here's the thrilling split-second finish that put the exclamation point on U.S. swimmer Michael Phelps' dazzling gold-medal run at the Beijing Olympics. The race was the 100-m butterfly, and as Phelps, on the left in this image, raced for his seventh gold medal, he lagged badly behind Serbian-American swimmer Milorad Cavic, who was swimming for Serbia, for most of the race. But as the two approached the finish, Phelps summoned his strength and took an extra half-stroke— a mistake, according to some experts. Mistake or not, Phelps surged forward and touched the wall .01 second ahead of his rival.

The Serb team quickly filed a protest, but after reviewing the official photographs, both the team and Cavic graciously accepted defeat. Veteran *Sports Illustrated* photographer Heinz Kluetmeier said of this image: "In terms of Olympic photos, it is near the top for me, because it defines a moment that a lot of people did not believe."

Jensen Beach, Fla., Aug. 19

Silver Lining

Not so long ago, the approach of September and the Labor Day holiday promised relief from the summer's heat for those living in hot climates. But these days, the last weeks of August are a time of anxiety, as Americans recall the four hurricanes that clobbered Florida in 2004 and the smackdown Hurricane Katrina dealt New Orleans in 2005. Now, as hurricane season begins, all eyes turn to the Atlantic, and sure enough, in 2008 a pair of tropical storms, Gustav and Ike, slammed into Caribbean islands and threatened the U.S. Gulf Coast. Gustav headed for New Orleans, but the storm ran out of power before it hit the mainland. Texans were not as lucky: Ike plowed into the Lone Star State, wreaking its worst havoc on Galveston Island.

Yet even such big blows can have a bright side. After Tropical Storm Fay flooded roads in one Florida town in August, local kids created a new sport: shoulder skiing.

Verbatim

QUOTES OF THE YEAR

MY OTHER RIDE IS A SPACE SHIP

MESSAGE on the airplane used by Richard Branson to reach the Mojave Desert, where the British billionaire unveiled the craft, left, that would provide the world's first commercial spaceflight

'I don't think riding in a fighter plane and getting shot down is a qualification to be President.'

WESLEY CLARK, on why John McCain's military service didn't make him more qualified than Barack Obama

'Is it not funny that those with 160,000 forces in Iraq accuse us of interference?'

MAHMOUD AHMADINEJAD, President of Iran, following the first visit to Iraq by an Iranian President since the 1980s

'Try to find another way to help or find your goal. This bomb, this weapons, it's not good to use it for anybody.'

OMAR BIN LADEN, a son of Osama bin Laden, calling for an end to the violence his father has inspired

'We don't have much. What we have in excess is women. So if you want them, we can give a few of those to you— some tens of thousands.'

MAO ZEDONG, China's onetime leader, attempting to barter the country's women during 1973 trade discussions with the U.S., according to a document released on Feb. 14 by the historian's office of the State Department

'My parents shut down Disneyland for me, so I'm good for a while.'

MILEY CYRUS, tween idol, on what she'd like for her sweet 16 after her parents threw her a birthday party at the famous theme park

'No person—not even Karl Rove—is above the law.'

U.S. HOUSE JUDICIARY CHAIRMAN JOHN CONYERS JR., after voting to cite Rove for defying a subpoena to testify about the firings of top Justice Department officials

'I didn't know you were Catholic.'

NANCY PELOSI, Speaker of the House, to Treasure Secretary Henry Paulson, after he went down on one knee to request her help in passing the $700 billion economic bailout package

'I'm not retiring until every American agrees with me.'

RUSH LIMBAUGH, conservative radio talk-show host, on his unprecedented new contract, estimated at $400 million

'I didn't take it very seriously. I guess everything the President does is interesting.'

GEORGE W. BUSH, who took a ribbing after U.S. Olympian Misty May-Treanor prodded him into patting her on the back for luck

'I want to give a shout-out to all my Saudi Arabian brothers and sisters. If you could all please send me some oil for my jet, I would truly appreciate it.'

SEAN (DIDDY) COMBS, hip-hop mogul, in a video blog, on the high cost of fuel. Combs added, "I can't believe I'm flying commercial"

'We did the essay, and that's what we did to win … We did whatever we could to win.'

PRISCILLA CEBALLOS, who in order to win Miley Cyrus/Hannah Montana concert tickets helped her 6-year-old daughter compose a fake essay about the girl's father dying in Iraq. The tickets were revoked

'Long before he was an actor or a governor, [he] wore little, tiny trunks and posed. He's a poser, and he should stop posing.'

LANCE CORCORAN, spokesman for the California Correctional Peace Officers Association, which launched a recall campaign against Governor Arnold Schwarzenegger, saying he mismanaged the state budget, resulting in a huge shortfall

'I've been hearing about his Senate speeches since I was in, like, the second grade.'

SARAH PALIN, Republican vice-presidential candidate, on Democratic rival Joe Biden

'For the first time, I realized he is an élitist.'

MAYHILL FOWLER, blogger for OffTheBus.net, who first reported on Barack Obama's comment at a San Francisco fund raiser that economic frustrations have made small-town Pennsylvania voters "bitter" and driven them to "cling to guns or religion"

'I think … I'll have my staff get back to you.'

JOHN MCCAIN, Republican presidential candidate, after being asked by a journalist how many homes he and wife Cindy, a multimillionaire heiress, own

'We had psychoanalytic sessions … Writing together with somebody is very intimate.'

MADONNA, on collaborating with Justin Timberlake on tracks for her new album, *Hard Candy*

'I very much like her hairdo. I took it as an inspiration. Because, in fact, it was also Brigitte Bardot's hairdo in the late '50s and '60s. And now Amy has made it her own style.'

KARL LAGERFELD, fashion designer, on Amy Winehouse's look

The World in 2008

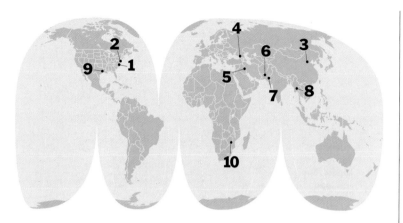

1 | Washington
U.S. Presidential Election

A race that began early in 2007 produced a pair of surprising nominees for the presidency. Seemingly out of the contest in the summer of 2007, Republican Senator John McCain of Arizona outlasted rivals, including Mitt Romney, Rudy Giuliani and Mike Huckabee—and the distaste of the party's strongly conservative base—to win the GOP nomination. Freshman Illinois Senator Barack Obama battled early front runner Senator Hillary Clinton until June before claiming the Democratic Party's nod. McCain threw a wild card into the race when he chose little-known Alaska governor Sarah Palin as his running mate. After the economy crashed in the fall, pocketbook worries became the defining issue of the campaign.

2 | Wall Street
Market Meltdown

"Wall Street got drunk," is how President George W. Bush described the genesis of the U.S. economic crash that engulfed the financial and banking industries and then spread to Main Street in 2008. It was the verdict on an era of lax regulation in which both bankers and consumers, lured by easy credit, racked up mountains of unsecured debt.

After the music finally stopped amid a national credit crunch, billions of dollars in wealth evaporated, a surprising number of financial institutions were destroyed or laid low, the government stepped in to shore up banks and insurance companies, and the economy wobbled on the brink of the worst disaster since the Great Depression.

3 | Beijing
2008 Olympics

China relished its role as host of the Summer Olympic Games, which it viewed as a tribute to its years of remarkable economic progress. Beijing was immensely proud of its athletes, who earned 51 gold medals, more than those of any other nation, and of the spectacular new architecture that dotted the city. But the Games' big stars were U.S. swimmer Michael Phelps, who won a record eight gold medals, and Jamaican sprinter Usain Bolt, shown, who won three.

4 | Caucasus
Russia Invades Georgia

Long-simmering tensions in the border region between Russia and Georgia boiled over in August when Moscow sent tanks and troops into the breakaway province of South Ossetia after Georgia attempted to assert control there. The short, brutal war left Georgia's military battered and its countryside ravaged—and put the world on notice that Vladimir Putin's Kremlin would aggressively project Russian power in the region.

Numbers:

9% Percentage of Americans who said they were satisfied with the country's direction in a fall '08 Gallup poll

13 Number of digits on Times Square's National Debt Clock, which ran out of space Sept. 30 when the U.S. debt reached $10 trillion

5 | Baghdad
The Surge Calms Iraq

The Bush Administration surge strategy that sent 30,000 additional U.S. troops to Iraq worked: in 2008 insurgent activity and sectarian violence sharply declined. The new approach was advocated and overseen by U.S. Army General David Petraeus, above. By the close of 2008 most of the extra troops had gone home, but the gains remained fragile and internal battles to control Iraq's future were still being fought.

The Administration argued that any further drawdown of American troops had to be weighed against the need to buy more time for the Iraqi state to take control of its ongoing problems of security, corruption and religious sectarianism. Another caveat: troops departing Iraq would likely be needed in Afghanistan, where the situation grew increasingly dire.

6 | Kabul
The Taliban Fights Back

Seven years after a U.S.-led war toppled the Taliban regime, resurgent Islamic militants—along with corruption, profits from illegal drugs and a weak central government —sent Afghanistan into a downward spiral. As the nation's security deteriorated, monthly casualty figures for U.S. service members in Afghanistan came to rival those in Iraq—even though there were only about a quarter the number of troops stationed there.

7 | Pakistan
The New Boss

After the assassination of popular politician Benazir Bhutto in the last days of 2007, Pakistan was plunged into turmoil. General turned President Pervez Musharraf, a U.S. ally, was forced to resign in August. The nation's new leader: Bhutto's controversial widower, Asif Ali Zardari, below.

8 | Burma
Cyclone Hits

An estimated 138,000 people were dead or missing after Cyclone Nargis plowed into Burma (Myanmar) on May 2, in the worst natural disaster in the nation's history. Yet just as appalling as the storm was the response of the nation's dictatorial and paranoid military regime, which refused to allow a host of international aid organizations to offer assistance, ensuring the doom of tens of thousands of citizens.

9 | United States
Natural Nightmares

Heavy spring rains fostered the worst flooding in the U.S. upper Midwest since 1993; hardest hit were Iowa, Indiana, Illinois and Missouri. During the late-summer tropical storm season, Hurricane Gustav threatened but spared New Orleans. But a stronger blow, Hurricane Ike, smashed into the Gulf Coast of Texas on Sept. 13, killing 72 people and flooding hard-hit Galveston Island, above.

10 | Zimbabwe
Mugabe Clings to Power

Robert Mugabe, 84, the former freedom fighter who led Rhodesia's drive to black rule, has become a corrupt dictator. In 2008 he held on to his grip on power by using the army to prevent his defeat in a general election, above—and later by refusing to abide by the terms of a power-sharing agreement he signed in September.

$1.5 BILLION Amount of money lost by Microsoft founder Bill Gates in the U.S. market crash, making Warren Buffet America's richest man

$1 Sale price of a foreclosed home in Detroit. The structure took 19 days to sell

'The new "real America"…is a place, finally, where the content of our President's character is more important than the color of his skin.'

—JOE KLEIN, *TIME* COLUMNIST

Election '08

Grant Park, Chicago, Nov. 4

Barack Obama's New America

The presidential election of 2008 was about much more than issues. It was the ratification of an essential change in the nature of the country. I've seen two others in my lifetime. The election of John Kennedy ratified the new America that had emerged from war and depression—a place where more people owned homes and went to college, a place where young people had the affluence to be idealistic or to rebel, a place that was safe enough to get a little crazy, a sexier country. Ronald Reagan's election was a rebellion against that—an announcement that toughness had replaced idealism overseas, that individual economic freedom had replaced common economic purpose at home. It was an act of nostalgia, harking back to the "real" America—white, homogeneous, small-town—that the '08 McCain campaign unsuccessfully tried to appeal to.

Democrat Barack Obama's victory creates the prospect of a new "real" America. We can't possibly know its contours yet, although I suspect the headline is that it is no longer homogeneous. It is no longer a "white" country, even though whites remain the majority. It is a place where the primacy of racial identity—and this includes the old, Jesse Jackson version of black racial identity—has been replaced by the celebration of pluralism, of cross-racial synergy. After eight years of misgovernance, the U.S. has lost some of its global swagger … but also some of its arrogance. It may no longer be as dominant, economically or diplomatically, as it once was. But it is younger, more optimistic, less cynical. It is a country that retains its ability to startle the world—and in a good way, with our freedom. It is a place, finally, where the content of our President's character is more important than the color of his skin. —BY JOE KLEIN

Victory! *Some 100,000 Chicagoans hail Obama's triumph on election night*

Yes, We Can!

Some princes are born in palaces, some in mangers. A few are born in the imagination, out of scraps of history and hope

BARACK OBAMA NEVER TALKS ABOUT HOW PEOPLE see him: I'm not the one making history, he said every chance he got. You are. Yet as he looked out on election night 2008 through the bulletproof glass, in a Chicago park named for a Civil War general, he had to see the truth on people's faces. We are the ones we've been waiting for, he liked to say, but people were waiting for him, waiting for someone to finish what a King began.

"If there is anyone out there who still doubts that America is a place where all things are possible," declared the President-elect, "who still wonders if the dream of our founders is alive in our time, who still questions the power of our democracy, tonight is your answer."

Barack Hussein Obama did not win because of the color of his skin. Nor did he win in spite of it. He won because at a very dangerous moment in the life of a still young country, more people than have ever spoken before came together to try to save it. And that was a victory all its own.

Remember this day, parents told their children as they took them out of school to go see an African-American candidate make history. An election in one of the world's oldest democracies looked like the kind they hold in brand-new ones, when citizens finally come out and dance, a purple-thumb day, a velvet revolution. A hundred thousand people came out in red states to hear Obama; a hundred fifty thousand turned out in purple ones, even after all this time, when they should have been sick to death of Hope and Change.

When it was over, more than 120 million pulled a lever or mailed a ballot, and the system could barely accommodate the demands of Extreme Democracy. Obama won more votes than anyone else in U.S. history, the biggest Democratic victory since Lyndon Johnson crushed another Arizona Senator 44 years before. Obama won men, which no Democrat had managed since Bill Clinton. He won 54% of Catholics, 66% of Latinos, 68% of new voters: a multicultural, multigenerational movement that shatters the old political ice pack. He let loose a deep blue wave that washed past the coasts and the college towns, into the South through Virginia and Florida, the Mountain West with Colorado and New Mexico, into the Ohio Valley and the Midwestern battlegrounds: you could almost walk from Maine to Minnesota without getting your feet wet in a red state. The victory poured down the ballot, bringing along a larger Democratic majority in both houses of Congress, though not as broad as some had predicted.

John McCain, freedom fighter and Obama's opponent, has always seen the nobility in battle, even—maybe especially—in a losing one, which takes the most courage to fight. When McCain called Obama to concede the race, the younger man honored the elder statesman. "I need your help," Obama said, and McCain offered it without reservation. "Whatever our differences, we are fellow Americans," McCain told the crowd in a gracious speech beneath the Arizona mountains. "I pledge to him tonight to do all in my power to help him lead us through the many challenges we face."

At a moment of obvious peril, America decided to place its fate in the hands of a man who had been born to an ide-

All smiles *Winning candidates Barack Obama and Joe Biden salute fans in Chicago's Grant Park on election night, Nov. 4*

alistic white teenage mother and the charismatic African grad student who abandoned them—a man who grew up without money, talked his way into good schools and excelled there, worked his way up through the pitiless world of Chicago politics to the U.S. Senate and now the White House in a stunningly short period. That achievement, compared with those of the Bushes or the Kennedys or the Roosevelts or the Adamses or any of the other American princes who were born into power or bred to it, represents such a radical departure from the norm that it finally brings meaning to the promise taught from kindergarten: "Anyone can grow up to be President."

Obama belonged to a party that was bent on retribution; he preached reconciliation. He had to build a new church and reach out to the seekers who had lost faith in government or never had any in the first place. We need to start over, he argued, speak gently, listen carefully, find solutions, keep our word. It was precisely because he was an outsider with a thin resumé and few cronies or scars or grudges that he could sell himself as the solution.

Beginning with his January 2008 victory in the Iowa caucuses, that's what he did. He won women without the help of women's groups, blacks without the help of race pols, and that golden snitch of American politics, the youth vote, whose presence not only gave his campaign a feeling of hope and energy but made old people feel younger too. That was the first test of what was really on voters' minds: even in the face of two wars and a looming recession, only 1 in 5 cited experience as the highest priority. More than a third of them cared most about who could bring about change.

Given a President who was radioactive and an economy weak in the knees, you could say the outcome should

Resolute *With running mate Sarah Palin at his side, John McCain delivers a heartfelt concession speech in Arizona*

Democratic Tide on the Hill

Riding Obama's coattails, Democrats increased their majority in both houses of Congress. The party gained at least 19 House seats and will effectively control at least 57 seats in the Senate, but three Senate races were undecided as of Nov. 6: Minnesota, Georgia and Alaska

WINNERS   LOSERS

KAY HAGAN (D)   **ELIZABETH DOLE** (R)

NORTH CAROLINA In a bitter contest, Hagan said incumbent Dole was ineffective, while Dole countered with a blistering attack on Hagan's supposed atheism

JEANNE SHAHEEN (D)   **JOHN SUNUNU** (R)

NEW HAMPSHIRE Both candidates were respected veterans who commanded devoted followers, but in a better year for Democrats, Shaheen triumphed

TWO UNDECIDED SENATE RACES AS OF 11/6/08

NORM COLEMAN (R)   **AL FRANKEN** (D)

MINNESOTA Incumbent Coleman's lead over Franken, a liberal radio host and former *Saturday Night Live* writer, was so slim it triggered an automatic recount

SAXBY CHAMBLISS (R)   **JIM MARTIN** (D)

GEORGIA Incumbent Chambliss came close to eking out a victory over Martin, but a runoff was scheduled for early December

never have been in doubt. Seventy percent more people voted in the Democratic primaries as in the Republican; 9 out of 10 people said the country was on the wrong track. In that light, McCain was his party's sacrificial lamb, a certified American hero granted one more chance to serve, with enough rebel credits on his resumé to stand a chance of winning over disgruntled voters if Obama imploded.

The Veep choice always promised to be complicated for a solo pilot who resisted the idea of a partner at every turn, but now the Constitution required him to pick a wingman. He wasn't the type to look for someone to help him govern. But what about someone to help him win?

In case anyone imagined that we'd make it through an entire general election without an all-out culture war, Sarah Palin's arrival took care of it. Alaska's governor called herself a fresh face who couldn't wait to take on the good ole boys. But far from framing the future, Palin played deep chords from the past—the mother of five from a frontier town who invoked the values of a simpler, safer America than the globally competitive, fiscally challenged, multicultural marketplace of ideas where Obama lived. She seemed to delight in the contrast: she was arguing that "we don't really know Barack Obama" before she had even taken off her coat. She warned urgently that he wasn't qualified to be President, even as leaders in her own party snorted at her lack of readiness; she rejoiced in visiting the "real America," the "pro-America areas of this great nation." Instead, it was an invitation for Obama to show how far the country had come. "There are no real or fake parts of this country," Obama fired back. "We are one nation, all of us proud, all of us patriots ..."

Still, as of mid-September, McCain, with Palin at his side, had closed the gender gap, ignited his base, delighted Rush Limbaugh and seemed to be having fun for the first time in ages. He hammered the point that he was the only one who had been tested in a crisis. It was working great— until he was tested in a crisis. It was Obama's triumph that the financial mess that might have buried him actually raised him up, let voters judge his judgment in real time, the 3 a.m. phone call that came night after night. It gave him, over the course of three weeks and three debates, a stage for statesmanship that decades of Senate debate could never have offered.

On the day Lehman Brothers evaporated, McCain was running 2 points ahead. In September, when the *Wall Street Journal* asked people who was better on taxes, McCain beat Obama, 41% to 37%. Over the next month, there was an 18-point swing, until Obama prevailed on taxes, 48% to 34%. The Obama campaign never missed a chance to replay McCain's quotes about the fundamentals of the economy being strong or that he was "fundamentally a deregulator" at a time when regulation was fundamentally overdue.

When McCain tried to seize the moment, suspend the campaign and ride back to Washington to rescue the global financial system only to be shut down by his own party, he handed Obama a weapon almost as powerful as the crisis itself. Times were suddenly scary—and McCain was "erratic," "impulsive," reckless. He fell into a trap he couldn't get out of for weeks: any attempt to do something dramatic and different just dug the hole deeper. Every time McCain took a swing, as his cheering section demanded he do, those undecided-voter dial meters plunged. Six in 10 voters said McCain was spending more time attacking Obama than explaining his own positions, in a time of crisis when people cared what those positions were.

Over the course of three debates right in the heat of the crisis, voters got to take the measure of the men directly—no stadium crowds, no stunts, no speechwriters to save them. They were being told that Obama was a dangerous radical who hung out with terrorists. Simply by seeming sober and sensible, he both reassured voters and diminished McCain, whose attacks suddenly seemed disingenuous. By mid-October, only 1 in 3 voters thought McCain would bring the country a real change in direction. He never got close again.

Eventually Obama's opponents moved past accusing him of celebrity and socialism to charging his family with witchcraft. Obama, meanwhile, used his immense financial advantage to run a half-hour prime-time ad that told his story, made his case—and never once mentioned McCain.

Far from framing the future, Palin played deep chords from the past

In a stern speech on election night, a victorious Obama challenged the nation: "This victory alone is not the change we seek. It is only the chance for us to make that change. And that cannot happen if we go back to the way things were. It cannot happen without you."

We get the leaders we deserve. And if we lift them up and then cut them off, refuse to follow unless they are taking us to Disneyland, then no President, however eloquent, however historic his mandate or piercing his sense of what needs to be done, can take us where we refuse to go. This did not all end on Election Day, Obama said again and again as he talked about the possibility of ordinary people doing extraordinary things. And so, we are merely at the end of the beginning.

—BY NANCY GIBBS

Sarah Palin. Conservative Republicans hail a new superstar from the north

America's second female vice-presidential candidate in history—and the first ever for the Republican Party—was a beauty contestant turned sportscaster turned governor of Alaska. But that's not all: Sarah Palin was also an anti-corruption crusader in an oil-soaked, scandal-racked state capital. A caribou hunter who showcased her femininity in fashion shoots. An Evangelical with very sharp elbows and worldly ambitions. And the mother of a child afflicted with Down syndrome. Her whirlwind introduction to the electorate was a succession of reactions: John McCain's Veep passed from surprise (who is this woman?) to scandal (her unmarried daughter's pregnant!) to obituary (will McCain drop her?) to resurrection (she's a pit bull with lipstick!) to skepticism (but can she appeal beyond the base?) at the speed of a racing snowmobile. But she embodied the basic American myth—Jefferson's yeoman farmer, the fantasia of rural righteousness—updated in a crucial way: now, Mom works too.

In choosing Palin, 44, McCain excited his party's socially conservative base, bolstered his standing in red states, put Democrats on the defensive and revolutionized the campaign narrative. But as the campaign progressed and polling numbers for the McCain-Palin ticket failed to catch fire beyond the party faithful, amid growing doubts that the novice on the national stage was up to the job of Vice President, a steady parade of prominent Republicans jumped ship. A civil war of anonymous quotes broke out within the McCain-Palin operation, and by the last weeks of the campaign, Palin had subtly started jockeying for advantage in the 2012 race for the GOP nomination.

How Obama Won

Riding a wave of new voters and responding to the economic concerns of older ones, he redraws the Democratic route to the White House

53%
Obama (D)
66,602,166 votes

46%
McCain (R)
58,236,089 votes

Others receiving votes:

Ralph Nader (I)	*698,564 votes*
Bob Barr (L)	*508,252 votes*
Chuck Baldwin (C)	*184,468 votes*

Behind the numbers

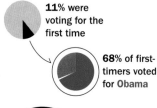

11% were voting for the first time

68% of first-timers voted for **Obama**

Economy 63%

The economy was the issue most important to voters

Iraq **10%**

Terrorism **9%**

Health Care **9%**

Energy **7%**

And **53%** of voters worried about the economy voted for **Obama**

Source: AP summary of national exit-poll data

Montana

McCain found himself in a surprisingly tough fight for Montana, but he kept the state in the red column, winning by about 12,000 votes

Helena — Billings

Missouri

Obama bracketed the state with wins in the population centers of St. Louis and Kansas City, but McCain won nearly everywhere else. Result: McCain clings to a 5,000-vote lead

Kansas City — Jefferson City — St. Louis

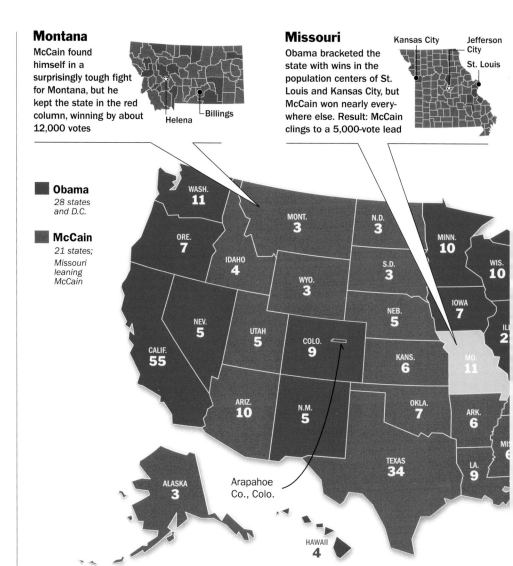

Obama
28 states and D.C.

McCain
21 states; Missouri leaning McCain

WASH. 11
ORE. 7
MONT. 3
N.D. 3
MINN. 10
IDAHO 4
WYO. 3
S.D. 3
WIS. 10
NEV. 5
UTAH 5
COLO. 9
NEB. 5
IOWA 7
ILL 2
CALIF. 55
KANS. 6
MO. 11
ARIZ. 10
N.M. 5
OKLA. 7
ARK. 6
ALASKA 3
TEXAS 34
LA. 9
MISS 6
HAWAII 4

Arapahoe Co., Colo.

How TIME's battleground counties voted

ARAPAHOE CO., COLO.
The Republican winning streak crashes to an end in this Denver suburb

Margin of victory (percentage points)

Obama +12
Dole +8.9
Bush +8
Bush +3.9
1996 2000 2004 **2008**

OAKLAND CO., MICH.
Jobs and the economy were prime concerns among voters, helping Obama reverse Democratic fortunes

Obama +14
Clinton +4.3
Gore +1.2
Kerry +0.5
1996 2000 2004 **2008**

HAMILTON CO., OHIO
This Cincinnati suburb, long a reliable Republican outpost, became a blue corner of the state for Obama

Dole +7
Bush +11.2
Bush +5.4
Obama +5
1996 2000 2004 **2008**

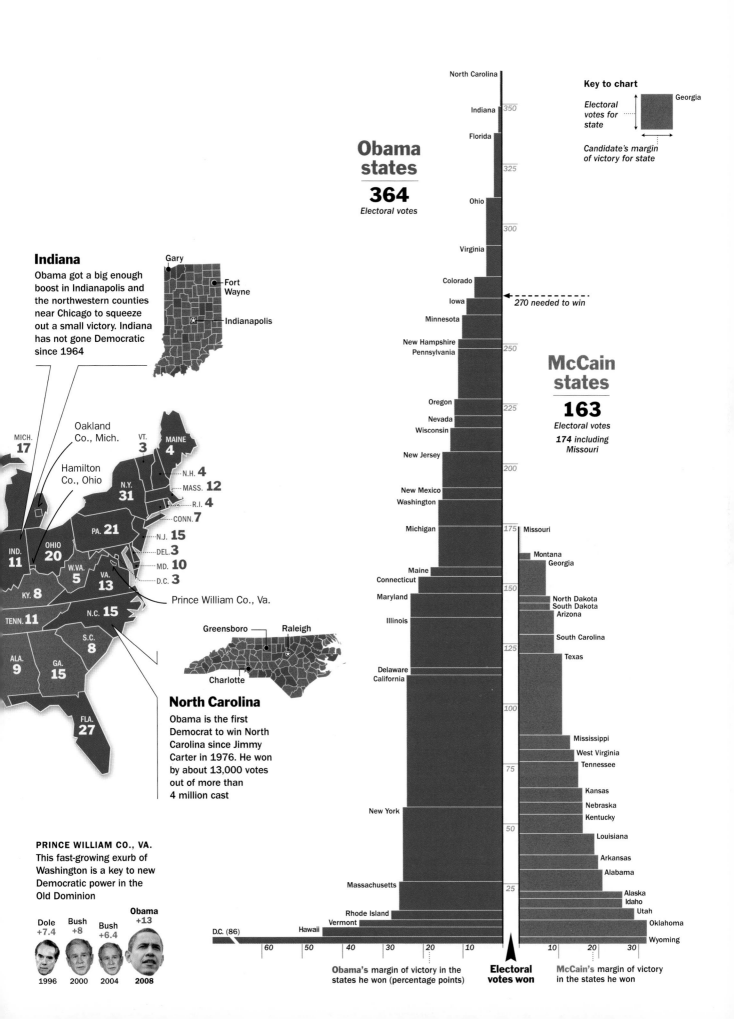

Key to chart

Electoral votes for state

Georgia

Candidate's margin of victory for state

Obama states
364
Electoral votes

North Carolina
Indiana
Florida
Ohio
Virginia
Colorado
Iowa
Minnesota
New Hampshire
Pennsylvania
Oregon
Nevada
Wisconsin
New Jersey
New Mexico
Washington
Michigan
Maine
Connecticut
Maryland
Illinois
Delaware
California
New York
Massachusetts
Rhode Island
Vermont
Hawaii
D.C. (86)

350 *325* *300* *275* *250* *225* *200* *175* *150* *125* *100* *75* *50* *25*

← - - - 270 needed to win

McCain states
163
Electoral votes
174 including Missouri

Missouri
Montana
Georgia
North Dakota
South Dakota
Arizona
South Carolina
Texas
Mississippi
West Virginia
Tennessee
Kansas
Nebraska
Kentucky
Louisiana
Arkansas
Alabama
Alaska
Idaho
Utah
Oklahoma
Wyoming

Indiana

Obama got a big enough boost in Indianapolis and the northwestern counties near Chicago to squeeze out a small victory. Indiana has not gone Democratic since 1964

Gary
Fort Wayne
Indianapolis

Oakland Co., Mich.

Hamilton Co., Ohio

MICH. **17**
VT. **3**
MAINE **4**
N.H. **4**
N.Y. **31**
MASS. **12**
R.I. **4**
CONN. **7**
PA. **21**
N.J. **15**
DEL. **3**
MD. **10**
D.C. **3**
OHIO **20**
IND. **11**
W.VA. **5**
VA. **13**
KY. **8**
N.C. **15**
TENN. **11**
S.C. **8**
ALA. **9**
GA. **15**
FLA. **27**

Prince William Co., Va.

Greensboro — Raleigh
Charlotte

North Carolina

Obama is the first Democrat to win North Carolina since Jimmy Carter in 1976. He won by about 13,000 votes out of more than 4 million cast

PRINCE WILLIAM CO., VA.
This fast-growing exurb of Washington is a key to new Democratic power in the Old Dominion

Dole **+7.4** — 1996
Bush **+8** — 2000
Bush **+6.4** — 2004
Obama +13 — **2008**

60 *50* *40* *30* *20* *10*   *10* *20* *30*

Obama's margin of victory in the states he won (percentage points)

Electoral votes won

McCain's margin of victory in the states he won

Backstage on The Hustings

Motto for the longest presidential campaign in U.S. history? *E pluribus duo*—out of many, two

Veterans *Above, Senator John McCain and his mother Roberta share a hug as they await returns from the South Carolina primary on Jan. 19. McCain won, and weeks later his mother celebrated her 96th birthday.*

A word? *On June 4, at the end of a long, bitter primary duel, Senator Hillary Clinton and presumptive Democratic nominee Barack Obama, left, share a private exchange after both spoke at a meeting of the American Israel Public Affairs Committee in the capital.*

Full-tilt *Former Arkansas governor and GOP candidate Mike Huckabee, right, keeps score in a game dating to Ronald Reagan's days on the stump: rolling an orange down the aisle of a campaign plane on takeoff.*

Java jive *Former New York City mayor Rudy Giuliani performs a standard rite of the campaign trail: acting nonplussed in a diner swarming with media. The day after this Jan. 29 visit to the Rascal House in Sunny Isles Beach, Fla., Giuliani placed third in the Florida GOP primary and withdrew from the race.*

Thanks! *At left, former Massachusetts governor Mitt Romney takes a congratulatory phone call from foe Mike Huckabee after winning the Michigan GOP primary on Jan. 15. Romney prevailed in 11 primaries and caucuses but was trailing John McCain in delegates after the Feb. 5 Super Tuesday primaries and withdrew from the race two days later.*

Are we there yet? *Below, Michelle Obama and daughters Malia, 10, at left, and Sasha, 7, join the man of the family as he stumps in Montana on the Fourth of July. Asked her main priority as First Lady by* TIME, *the candidate's wife said she hoped she could give her children a normal upbringing in the White House.*

On the road again *There are enough storylines to fill a Tolstoy novel in the quiet picture above, taken aboard John McCain's campaign bus on Aug. 29. At left, McCain's surprising and controversial choice for running mate, Alaska Governor Sarah Palin, feeds her son Trig, a special-needs child who was born on April 18. At right is campaign manager Steve Schmidt, an acolyte of George W. Bush's longtime political aide Karl Rove, who brought Rove's hard-driving style to the campaign. The Senator's wife Cindy has a brace on her right arm, after one too many vigorous handshakes along the rope lines of the campaign trail.*

Aisles of smiles *At left, Democratic candidate and 2004 vice-presidential nominee John Edwards is hailed in Cedar Rapids while campaigning in Iowa. After an early string of losses, Edwards withdrew from the race on Jan. 30. In August he confirmed reports that he and a former campaign worker had an extramarital affair.*

Chill out! *Here's a bracing reminder of how long U.S. presidential campaigns have become: by the time these folks braved the elements to support Hillary Clinton in Vinton, Iowa, on Dec. 30, 2007, she had been runnng for the Oval Office for 11 months, and there were 11 more months to go before the general election.*

Steak break *John McCain enjoys a respite from the grueling campaign grind at his ranch outside Sedona, Ariz., on Aug. 23. In a classic campaign gaffe, McCain, whose wife Cindy is the heir to a beer-distributing fortune, was unable to recall how many houses the couple owned when asked by a reporter.*

Chin up! *Amid the dull routine of life on the campaign trail, Barack Obama does an impromptu pull-up to stay in shape. The disciplined fitness buff set aside 45 minutes at the start of most days for working out. Scouting report on the candidate: dangerous with a basketball, dreadful with a bowling ball.*

Just folks *Below, Todd Palin, husband of the GOP vice-presidential candidate, eyes* TIME *photographer Christopher Morris at an ice-cream stand in New Concord, Ohio. Sarah Palin is at right, and the McCains are waiting for their treat at the window.*

Hillary! *Senator Clinton takes the stage at a March 24 rally in Uniontown, while campaigning in the Pennsylvania Democratic primary. The former First Lady entered the campaign as the frontrunner, but on Jan. 3, Barack Obama won the first major contest of the campaign, the Iowa caucuses. Five days later, the gritty Clinton came back to beat Obama in New Hampshire, despite polls that showed him leading. A long, grueling, seesaw campaign followed, and Clinton did not concede the party's nomination to Obama until early in June.*

Heartland *At top right, Republican voters attend a McCain-Palin rally in Lebanon, Ohio, on Sept. 9, at which both candidates appeared. Palin, a working mother of five children—the youngest of whom, Trig, was born in April 2008 with Down syndrome—was a favorite of GOP women. By the end of the race, when the two candidates most often campaigned separately, Palin's rallies consistently drew larger crowds than McCain's.*

All-around appeal *Photographer Brooks Kraft captured a panoramic image of Barack Obama speaking to a crowd in Leesburg, Va., on Oct. 22. An estimated 35,000 people attended the event in the longtime Republican-leaning state, and on Nov. 4 the Illinois Senator became the first Democrat to carry the Old Dominion since 1964.*

LEFT: DIANA WALKER FOR TIME; RIGHT: BROOKS KRAFT—CORBIS; BOTTOM: BROOKS KRAFT—CORBIS

Nation

The Great Wall of America

After years of acrimonious debate, in 2007 Congress allocated $1.2 billion to the building of a fence that one day may stretch across the entire border between the U.S. and Mexico, and the Department of Homeland Security (DHS) promptly started hiring posthole diggers. DHS hopes to complete more than 650 miles (roughly 1,000 km) of barrier by the end of 2008. So far, progress has been fastest in California and Arizona. At right is a section of the fence outside San Luis, Ariz.: the U.S. is on the left; Mexican land and factories are on the right. U.S. authorities say the double barrier and buffer zone, along with increased surveillance, have substantially reduced local illegal crossings.

TIME's David von Drehle noted, "What tastes like common sense to one voter—cracking down on illegal crossings—smacks of xenophobia to the next, and the same rumble of helicopters and border-patrol Jeeps in the Southwestern desert sounds to some people like America standing up for itself but to others like Emma Lazarus, poet of the Statue of Liberty, rolling over in her grave."

Henry Paulson. George W. Bush's third Secretary of the Treasury reaped the whirlwind of an economy in free-fall

LATE IN THE SUMMER OF 2008, TREASURY SECRETARY Henry Paulson shared the secret of his success with a TIME journalist: "You define your job expansively." The man practices what he preaches. Lured to Treasury in the summer of 2006 by a President in need of domestic-policy credibility, Paulson grabbed the rudder of a $14 trillion national economy churning its way through a maelstrom.

The 6-ft. 1-in. former Dartmouth football star, 62 in 2008, came to the Bush Administration after spending seven years as CEO of Goldman Sachs, the current cream of Wall Street firms. The key to his approach was that he spent the bulk of his career not as a manager but as an investment banker, a master of building relationships with CEOs and other stakeholders in a deal.

Paulson showed his dealmaking powers at the highest level when he won quick passage of a massive housing bill in late July 2008 over the objections of many GOP lawmakers and even some White House aides. But in October he proved a poor pitchman for his proposed $700 billion economic bailout package; his public warnings that disaster was imminent but that the evidence had to remain secret were reminiscent

of antiterrorism officials who raised the threat level to orange but wouldn't tell us why.

Paulson and Bush failed to brand the package as an economic recovery plan instead of a bailout. They began by demanding almost Napoleonic levels of authority, although they later compromised on that. They released the $700 billion figure without making clear that Treasury could eventually get most of the money back if the economy rebounded. And they didn't make the case until all was nearly lost that the credit crunch endangered loans for cars, homes, farms and businesses—which in turn endangered millions of jobs and pensions. "I begged them to explain this to the guy on his couch, and they never did," said Congressman Steve LaTourette, an Ohio Republican. Result: the House voted it down, and it wasn't until the stock market swooned that average investors realized they had a stake in the package, and it passed.

In an interview with TIME, Paulson agreed that "we just haven't communicated as well as we need to." Perhaps. Or perhaps the credibility problems were more about the messengers than the message.

—BY JUSTIN FOX AND MICHAEL GRUNWALD

Ben Bernanke. The Federal Reserve chief pledged his allegiance to Alan Greenspan—before the meltdown

WHAT A DIFFERENCE THREE YEARS MAKE: IN 2005, when President Bush chose the White House's relatively new top economic adviser to succeed Alan Greenspan as chairman of the Federal Reserve, Ben Bernanke professed alignment with the Maestro. The "top priority," he said, will be to "maintain continuity" with Greenspan's way of doing things. Then history intervened, in the form of the subprime-mortgage crisis that erupted in 2007 and the credit melt-down that followed. Since then, the Fed chief has earned the nickname "Helicopter Ben," because of his belief that it's the government's job to litter the landscape with money, if necessary, to prevent economic collapse.

Faced with the worst U.S. financial crisis since the Depression, Bernanke went to unprecedented lengths to keep things from getting worse. In March, the Fed forced and helped finance a shotgun marriage between about-to-fail investment bank Bear Stearns and JPMorgan Chase. Later in the year, Bernanke endorsed Treasury's plan to inject capital directly into the banks and backed multiple stimulus packages for the economy.

Bernanke's aggressive intervention was strongly at odds with Greenspan's frequent admonitions to let financial firms take care of themselves, but even Bernanke's predecessor admitted to a House committee in late October that the Fed should have regulated them more firmly. By the end of 2008, Bernanke had been imitating Jimmy Stewart in *It's a Wonderful Life* and trying to halt bank runs for more than a year. But while Stewart's George Bailey had to make do with his powers of persuasion and his honeymoon fund to save the Bailey Building & Loan, Bernanke had the full faith and credit of the U.S. government behind him. He also had a delicate balance to maintain: too far in one direction, and he would bail out all the irresponsible people and institutions that had caused the subprime mess and sub-sequent debt-market crunch. Too far in the other, and the global financial system could collapse on his watch.

Early in his career as an economist, the South Carolina-raised and Harvard- and MIT-educated Bernanke, 55, studied the causes of the Great Depression and conclud-ed that the "malfunctioning of financial institutions" was a major culprit. A quiet academic who later chaired Princeton's economics department, Bernanke is differ-ent from Greenspan (whose tortured, Delphic utter-ances became legendary) in another crucial respect: he believes in being direct. "Stabilization of the financial markets is a critical first step," he said in an October speech. "But even if they stabilize as we hope they will, broader economic recovery will not happen right away."

—BY DANIEL KADLEC AND JUSTIN FOX

By the end of 2008, Bernanke was imitating Jimmy Stewart in *It's a Wonderful Life*

Michael Bloomberg. New York City's visionary mayor has shown that our urban spaces can be both great and green

I HAVE LONG ARGUED THAT ONE OF OUR MOST CRITICAL environmental issues is the challenge of making our cities attractive, enriching and safe places to live. The best cure for destructive sprawl is to build cities people don't want to abandon, places where they can live healthy, fulfilling lives in densities that don't devour our landscapes, pave our wilderness and pollute our watersheds, air and wildlife. To achieve this, we need to invest in urban schools, transportation, parks, health care, police protection and infrastructure that makes cities great magnets with gravity sufficient to draw back the creeping suburbs.

There is a moral as well as an environmental impera- tive to attend to landscapes that are home to so many. For more than 8 million New York City residents, the environment is not a Rocky Mountain meadow with pronghorns grazing beside an alpine stream. It's their transit system and office buildings, the parks where their children play.

No one understands this better than New York City's mayor, Michael Bloomberg, 66, who has not only worked to make his city livable but has also promised to make it a global model of sustainability. Mayor

Bloomberg realizes that a better future for New York will not be constructed on jobs or housing alone. It must also include cleaner air, safer drinking water, more green spaces and a healthy, accessible Hudson River.

In addition to protecting the local environment, he has promised to make New York a paradigm in the fight against global warming. His visionary PlaNYC commits New York to plant 1 million trees, slash greenhouse gases 30% by 2030 and achieve the cleanest air of any big city on the continent. Mayor Bloomberg has stepped into the breach left by a Federal Government that has abdicated all leadership on global warming. With his pragmatism and boundless energy, he has shown that a city can be both great and green. If that idea can make it here, it can make it anywhere.

—BY ROBERT F. KENNEDY JR.

Kennedy is senior attorney for the Natural Resources Defense Council, whose headquarters are in New York City

[Editors' note: Bloomberg, New York City's mayor since 2001, disavowed previous statements on Oct. 2 and declared he would seek to have the city's term-limits law revised, enabling him to run for a third term.]

Eliot Spitzer. New York's steamrolling governor, once touted as presidential timber, has a great fall

HIS VISAGE DESCRIBED DISCOUNTENANCE." ELIOT Spitzer wrote those words about a character in a short story for his high school literary magazine. The sentence was florid in an adolescent way—Spitzer was always something of an intellectual show-off. But Spitzer's rather poetic sentence seemed apt on March 12, as he resigned as governor of New York in a brief press conference, the culmination of a 48-hour melodrama sparked by revelations that he had been a client of a prostitution ring.

Thus ended a public career that had once seemed so promising that Spitzer was discussed as a potential 2012 Democratic presidential nominee. Spitzer apologized for his "private failings," but he said nothing to explain why he would have thrown it all away, why he risked so much. He had built a reputation as an ethical crusader, and as a former prosecutor, he knew well the myriad electronic and surveillance tools that reveal hidden arrangements for crimes like prostitution. In 2007, Spitzer had signed a law that lengthened jail time for johns from three months to as much as a year.

How does a man like this expect not to be caught? Although Spitzer had never before shown signs of a personal temperament that ran to the louche, he had a long history of recklessness, a sense that the usual boundaries of authority didn't apply to him. Part of it was being not just the brilliant son of a multimillionaire—someone who surely sensed entitlement from an early age—but the son of a particular multimillionaire, New York City real estate developer Bernard Spitzer, a fierce, demanding parent.

Eliot Spitzer always had a complex relationship with authority. As attorney general of New York—the position he held for eight years before winning the governorship—he made a name for himself by aggressively prosecuting Wall Street fraud;

TIME called him "Crusader of the Year" in 2002. But many on Wall Street felt he went too far, pressuring ethically wayward but not necessarily criminal companies into agreeing to unfairly large settlements by threatening their CEOs with prolonged legal battles.

Spitzer's approval ratings plummeted after his election; it didn't help that not long after becoming governor, Spitzer said to the Republican leader in the state assembly, "I'm a f_____ steamroller, and I'll roll over you." Like many scolds, Spitzer seemed to believe his burning pursuit of right justified any personal failings—his boorishness, the overweening use of his offices and, one presumes, his philandering.

—BY JOHN CLOUD

How does a man like this expect not to be caught?

Farewell, Free Lunch

Welcome to the deleveraging of America, as a bubble economy based on debt and denial finally collides with reality, and both Wall Street and Main Street face hard times

TUMULTUOUS PERIODS OF FINANCIAL BOOM and bust come to be defined by a word or catchphrase. Tulipmania. The Great Depression. The dotcom bubble. The word that could define the financial times Americans are now living through—and the economic pain that began rocking the nation in 2008— is *leverage*.

Leverage was the mother's milk of Wall Street and of Main Street for the past 20 years. Leverage meant debt, specifically the number of dollars you could borrow for every dollar of wealth you had. It meant borrowing other people's money to invest in something you wanted to invest in, or to buy something you wanted to buy. On Wall Street, debt funded investments in pretty much every sort of thing a financial firm could bet on, including the toxic mortgage-backed securities that led the way into this crisis. On Main Street, it meant borrowing to buy a house or condo—maybe two—then perhaps borrowing again off the increasing value of that property to pay for something else: a flat-screen TV, a new set of golf clubs, your daughter's braces.

Our debt binge was fueled by easy money and the belief that prices of assets—those houses in particular—never went down: only interest rates did. That era is over. It will be replaced by what will be one of the more painful and consequential, economic chapters in our history: the great *deleveraging* of America.

The first domino of the crisis fell in the summer of 2007, when two mortgage funds operated by investment bank Bear Stearns became insolvent. This led to a broader shakeout in the market for subprime mortgages as a whole, and that sparked a credit crisis: as the market for mortgage securities dried up, other credit markets followed suit. All of these events set the stage for a more fundamental, economy-wide series of shocks in 2008.

Throughout the year, each week conjured another financial horror show, as if Stephen King were channeling Alan Greenspan to produce scary stories full of negative numbers. As the months ticked by, the basic pattern remained the same. Financial tizzy. Dramatic government action. Period of reduced tizzy. Repeat.

In March, Bear Stearns avoided collapse by merging with JPMorgan Chase & Co., at the behest of newly engaged federal regulators. In June, Fannie Mae and Freddie Mac started to teeter. Their fall would have been a calamity: the two publicly traded, government-chartered companies, along with

Perfect storm *At top left, consumers paid all-time high prices for gas over the summer, but, if painful, that boost was not related to the economy's fundamental woes. At top right, workers leave the IndyMac Bank after its collapse; a Wall Street trader feels the pain; and the most visible and pervasive symbol of the housing collapse, a foreclosure sign*

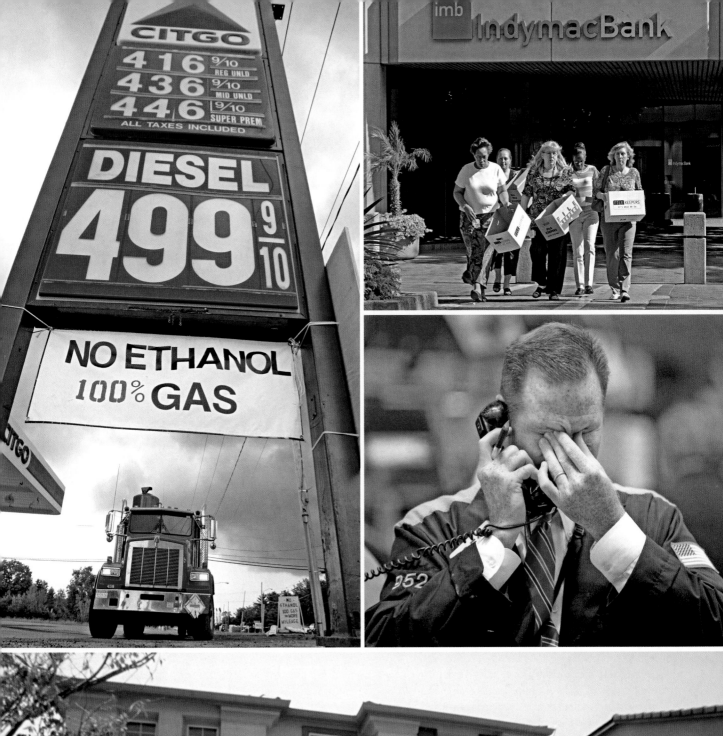

Sign of the times *Dana Blumenthal of Brooklyn joins protesters on Wall Street in New York City on Sept. 25 to demonstrate against the proposed federal bailout of financial institutions*

the Federal Housing Administration, had been almost entirely responsible for sustaining mortgage-lending in the U.S. since the market for private mortgage-backed securities collapsed in the summer of 2007. Their viability was important because, together, the two companies held or guaranteed about half the nation's mortgage loans.

But this worry was temporarily eclipsed by a more urgent disaster. In July, the largest-ever U.S. thrift failure was revealed as federal banking officials seized California-based IndyMac Bank, after it proved unable to withstand the perfect storm of tighter credit, falling home prices and rising foreclosures. By the end of that month, however, Fannie and Freddie were back in the spotlight: the Treasury's willingness to backstop the companies, which together were on the hook for $5.2 trillion in mortgage debt (just slightly less than the entire U.S. federal debt), began to raise concerns about the fundamental soundness of T-bills and bonds. These concerns were laid to rest (at least for the short run) on Sept. 7, when federal authorities seized control of both the stagering mortgage giants.

One week later, however, federal officials refused to rescue the embattled Lehman Brothers investment bank. During a dramatic series of weekend negotiations, these same officials arranged a shotgun marriage of Merrill Lynch (which they feared would be brought down by the aftershocks of Lehman's failure) to the Bank of America. Just 48 hours later, federal officials hastily cobbled together a $85 billion rescue package to prop up the distressed insurance giant, AIG.

Along the way, the last two major independent investment banks, Goldman Sachs and Morgan Stanley, agreed

This effectively spelled the end of a decades-long era in which swashbuckling bankers were free to leverage themselves to the hilt

Wipeout *A trader at the New York Mercantile Exchange reels as prices fall on Sept. 16. It got worse: weeks later, with the markets in the grip of a selling fever, some $6.5 trillion in global losses were racked up in only two days, Oct. 6 and 7*

to become commercial bank holding companies—a move that brought greater financial protection from the government, along with greater regulatory oversight. This effectively spelled the end of a decades-long era in which swashbuckling bankers were free to leverage themselves to the hilt and put down the kind of hyper-aggressive bets that could yield stunning returns in good times but lead to staggering losses in bad times.

In the harrowing weeks that followed these developments, another bank—Washington Mutual, the nation's largest savings and loan—was seized by federal regulators and another reeling financial giant, Wachovia, was married off to a Wells Fargo, a suitor with a better balance sheet, at the urging of government officials.

The Bailout Bounces Back

AS EQUITY MARKETS ROILED AND CREDIT MARKETS SEIZED up, Washington went to the well once more, as a lame-duck President and his economic team joined Democrat-

ic and Republican congressional leaders to ask Americans to trust them with a $700 billion Wall Street rescue package advocated by Treasury Secretary Henry Paulson. The plan was immediately tagged a "bailout," perhaps dooming its chances to pass Congress. For the well of public trust had long run dry. Outraged calls overwhelmed Capitol Hill switchboards, and on Sept. 29, despite bipartisan backing and the reluctant buy-in of both presidential candidates, the huge bailout plan failed in the House.

After the vote, the Administration found a new and much more effective spokesman for its case that Wall Street chaos was bad for everyone: the Dow Jones industrial average plunged 778 points, and suddenly Main Street was calling for help. By the first week in October, Congress had passed (and the President had signed) TARP, the Troubled Asset Relief Program. The measure, still carrying a $700 billion pricetag, was originally intended to shore up the balance sheets of banks by purchasing their distressed securities. But the damage continued to mount:

Under fire *President Bush joins his economic advisers at the White House on Sept. 19 to call for Congress to pass the $700 billion bailout package. From left, Federal Reserve Chairman Bernanke, Bush, Treasury Secretary Paulson and Securities and Exchange Commission Chairman Christopher Cox*

by mid-month, a global stock-market rout had swallowed 18% of the Dow. Within two weeks, Treasury Department officials had been forced to reimagine TARP to allow government purchases of stock in leading banks. Paralleling a successful program authored by British Prime Minister Gordon Brown, it called for the U.S. government to take partial ownership of nine leading banks and offer to buy pieces of hundreds of others.

On Oct. 13, the nine bank bosses, assembled in the Treasury's imposing boardroom, were each handed a piece of paper with the terms: $25 billion of preferred shares each from Citigroup, JPMorgan Chase, Wells Fargo and Bank of America. In return for the capital, the U.S. would collect a 5% dividend in the first five years. Although Wells Fargo chairman Richard Kovacevich resisted, Paulson gave the bankers no choice. It amounted to partial nationalization, although in announcing the bailout on Oct. 14, Paulson deliberately avoided using that term. "Today's actions are not what we ever wanted to do, but today's actions are what we must do to restore confidence in our financial system," he said.

How We Got Here

1. **The Bubble Bursts**
Housing values fall as supply overwhelms demand. Many subprime borrowers find that their homes are worth less than their mortgages. Defaults rise, sending prices south. The downward spiral begins.

2. **Run of CDOs**
Investors pile into collateralized debt obligations (CDOs), which are complicated securities based on pools of mortgages. CDOs are often (absurdly) rated AA and AAA and are considered as safe as Treasury bonds.

3. **Leverage Loves Company**
Firms borrow to load up on CDOs and real estate. Lehman Brothers was leveraged more than 30 to 1. AIG sells credit-default swaps (CDSs), derivatives designed to protect investors from failures.

4. **The Mortgage Collapse**
Consumers who got big mortgages with little documentation begin to default. Lenders like Washington Mutual and Countrywide Financial see their stock prices sink. Fiscal comeuppance rears its ugly head.

5. **Finance Takes The Next Hit**
Rising delinquencies mean that CDOs lose value. The investment banks must take write-downs and raise capital; the rout begins. Bear Stearns goes down. Lehman Brothers plays an endgame and loses.

No Fuel, No Rocket

AS THE DELEVERAGING TOOK HOLD, MILLIONS OF AMERI-cans found the prospect of living within their means growing meaner by the day. Its consequences began showing in the bankruptcies of retailers such as Linens 'n Things, Mervyns, Steve & Barry's, Shoe Pavilion, Goody's and Sharper Image and in the possibility of poor holiday sales. The overleveraged consumer was now the biggest economic problem facing the country, because debt has been the rocket fuel that has propelled growth for most of the past decade. Two-thirds of the $14 trillion U.S. economy is driven by consumer spending, and the relentless shop-per has also been critical to the growth in once booming exports led by economies like China's.

American consumers had become more addicted to debt than Wall Street was. Total household debt at the end of 2007 was $13.8 trillion, up 20% since 2005. At the same time, the household savings rate ticked down close to zero; the rocket's engine was running on empty.

Everywhere, in the fall of 2008, consumers were reeling: cashing out 401(k)s, cutting back on spending, cutting up credit cards and using only debit cards and cash. For a U.S. company in retail—the country's second largest industry, employing some 25 million Americans—those are about the most depressing words you can hear. The great risk, as consumers cut their spending, was that bad economic news begets more bad news. In late October Federal Reserve Chairman Ben Bernanke called this the "adverse-reaction loop": as consumers spend less, the economy weakens more, so unemployment rises and mortgage foreclosures increase, putting more pressure on the financial system—and on the downward spiral goes.

That widening gyre is what the government was trying to avoid at all costs. "We're going to see an evaporation of concern about fiscal restraint simply because the threat of an economic collapse is so great," said Robert Reis-chauer, president of the Urban Institute, a public-policy think tank. In other words, as the real world sheds debt, the government will take on more and more in the hope that at some point the economy will stabilize and then be-gin growing again.

'Today's actions are not what we ever wanted to do ... but ... are what we must do.'

—TREASURY'S HENRY PAULSON

The good news is that most economists believe all the weaponry the government is throwing at the problem will eventually have an effect. Interest rates are low and probably headed lower. More fiscal stimulus is on the way. Many economists are currently forecasting a couple of quarters of outright economic contraction. But many see a resumption of slow growth by the second half of 2009. The sky, in other words, is not necessarily falling. But as of November 2008, it sure looked that way.

—BY BILL POWELL, MICHAEL GRUNWALD AND TIME STAFF

What's Next

6. Begin the Bailout
Fannie and Freddie have to be made federal wards to try to stop the crisis. Wishful thinking. Next, the Fed steps in to save AIG before rolling out a $700 billion bailout. The markets weaken with worry.

7. The Freeze
Some credit markets seize up, including auction-rate securities, hurting municipalities. Large banks get skittish. Spreads on junk bonds and even better-rated corporate bonds are widening. This raises costs for businesses.

8. The Market Gets Volatile
Volatility is bad for the stock market, and indicators are off the charts. Investors head to the sidelines, willing to park their money in three-month Treasuries at less than 1% interest until it's safe to come out.

9. The Deleveraging Death Spiral
Banks under stress, like Washington Mutual and Wachovia, need to set aside more capital against potential losses. So they have to sell assets, which drives asset prices even lower, which requires more capital. Repeat.

10. Wall Street to Main Street
As lending tightens, short-term loans on which all kinds of businesses rely become less available. The negative potential is huge: if the gears of commerce get stuck, growth slows and layoffs follow as cost-cutting ensues.

Briefing

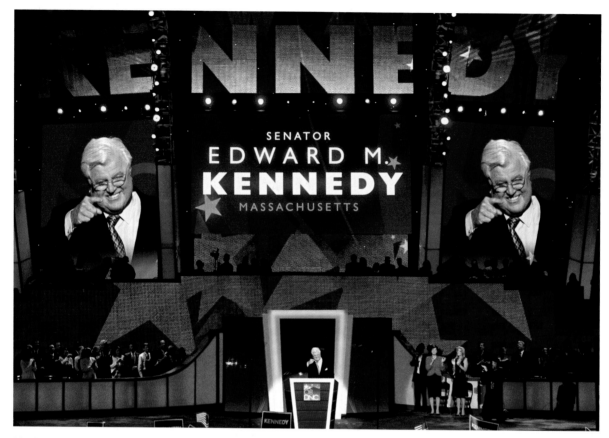

Lion's roar *An ailing Senator Ted Kennedy of Massachusetts rouses delegates at the Democratic National Convention on Aug. 25 in Denver. In May, Kennedy announced that doctors had found he suffered from a malignant glioma, a cancerous brain tumor. Later, Senator John McCain hailed Kennedy in a presidential debate as "the lion of the Senate."*

Feeling the Heat. A disgraced former pro athlete, the mayor of Detroit, and Alaska's popular senior Senator are in the spotlight, for all the wrong reasons

1. O.J. Simpson *The onetime football great was acquitted of murdering his wife Nicole and her friend Ronald Goldman in a 1995 trial that riveted the nation. He was later found liable for the deaths in a civil case. On Oct. 3, 13 years to the day after he was found not guilty in his criminal case, a Las Vegas jury began deliberating on whether Simpson, 61, was guilty of charges of armed robbery and the kidnapping of two sports memorabilia dealers in the Palace Station casino-hotel in 2007. Simpson's friend Clarence (C.J.) Stewart was a co-defendant. Four other men involved in the scheme to retrieve items of Simpson memorabilia had earlier pled guilty and testified against the two. On Oct. 6 both defendants were found guilty. Simpson is due to be sentenced in December 2008; he could face life in prison.*

2. Kwame Kilpatrick *Detroit's mayor, 38, faced a slate of criminal charges stemming from his affair with a co-worker and attempts to cover it up. He was accused of perjury and assaulting a county investigator; he spent a night in jail for violating bail conditions; he was ordered to wear an electronic tether and was ordered to take a drug test. On Sept. 4 he signed a plea bargain under which he agreed to resign his office, plead guilty to two counts of criminal obstruction of justice, pay $1 million restitution and spend four months in jail.*

3. Ted Stevens *Alaska's senior Senator, 84—after 40 years in office, a respected voice on Capitol Hill—was indicted on charges of corruption and went on trial in a Washington, D.C., courtroom on Sept. 24. He was charged with knowingly failing to disclose on Senate financial forms more than $250,000 in work done on his Alaska home and other gifts he received from VECO Corp., a powerful oil-pipeline contractor. On Oct. 27, a jury convicted Stevens on each of seven counts. He vowed to appeal the verdict and continue his 2008 bid for re-election.*

Anthrax: Case Closed?

On Aug. 6, nearly seven years after anonymous letters containing anthrax spores killed five people and sickened 17 others, the FBI and the Department of Justice presented their case against Bruce Ivins, 62, a researcher at the U.S. Army Medical Research Institute for Infectious Diseases in Maryland. The suicide of Ivins on July 29 forced the feds to go public with their case against him before it was ready. Even so, the evidence they released was compelling: records showed Ivins worked

late at the lab on the nights leading up to the anthrax mailings, and e-mails he sent at the time showed signs of extreme mental distress.

Since Ivins' death, his attorney, Paul Kemp, has repeatedly said he was innocent and claims Ivins fully cooperated with the FBI during two dozen interviews and passed at least two lie-detector tests. Kemp claims the FBI harassed his client for months, driving him into a suicidal spiral of alcohol and depression.

Court Backs Gitmo Detainees

Rebuking Bush Administration policies, the Supreme Court ruled on June 12 that foreign terrorism suspects held at Guantánamo Bay have the right to challenge their detention without being charged in federal district courts. The 5-to-4 decision (swing vote: Justice Anthony Kennedy) marked the fourth time the court ruled against Administration attempts to create a separate legal framework for holding and prosecuting Gitmo detainees. In a scathing dissent, Justice Antonin Scalia warned that the nation "will live to regret what the court has done today."

Fast Track to Tragedy

In the deadliest U.S. rail accident in 15 years, a Los Angeles Metrolink commuter train plowed into a Union Pacific freight train on Sept. 12, killing 25 people and injuring at least 130, many severely. But there was more to the story: the crash may have been due to operator error. Metrolink engineer Robert Sanchez, 46, sent a text message only 22 seconds before the trains collided, National Transportation Safety Board investigators said in October. The calamity boosted calls to provide additional federal funding to enhance safety technology on U.S. rail lines.

Since You Asked ...

Nancy Pelosi. The controversial Speaker of the House replies to our readers' queries

The Democratic Congress is perceived by the public to have accomplished almost nothing. What do you say to this?

Kyle Victor Stich, CHICAGO

We raised the minimum wage, made college more affordable with the biggest bill since the GI Bill was signed in 1944, passed a historic energy bill with emission standards. But we didn't end the war, and I think that's why people have a negative view of Congress.

Why do you focus so much on deriding the President? Wouldn't it be better to just debate the issues?

Jeffrey Kraker, COLUMBIA, MD.

I rarely make personal attacks on the President. He's an amiable fellow. But he's done tremendous harm. There isn't any subject that you can name that hasn't been severely damaged by the policies of the Bush Administration.

Will you see the day when a woman becomes President?

Liz Gonzalez, SANGER, CALIF.

I'm counting on it. It could be soon. But it's only a matter of time.

World

Man Without a Country

Though reigning in exile, the Dalai Lama is by now the most seasoned ruler on the planet, having led his people for 68 years—longer than Queen Elizabeth II, King Bhumibol Adulyadej of Thailand or even Fidel Castro. By Tibetan custom he is regarded as the incarnation of a god, the god of compassion. His occupied land certainly needed compassion in 2008, as freedom demonstrations against Chinese rule began in March and fostered some of the bloodiest confrontations since similar protests led to a brutal crackdown in the late 1980s. This year's violence left as many as 140 Tibetans dead.

In his exile home in the northern India hill station of Dharamsala, the Dalai Lama, as a Buddhist monk, speaks unstintingly on behalf of all people's rights to basic freedoms of speech and thought—though as a Buddhist monk, he also holds staunchly to the view that violence can never solve a problem deep down. "Genuine harmony must come from the heart," the monk told TIME contributor Pico Iyer. "It cannot come from the barrel of a gun."

Ingrid Betancourt. She endured more than six years of hell. Is there a second act for the celebrated hostage?

IN THE FIRST WEEKS AFTER SHE EMERGED FROM SIX and a half harrowing years as a FARC hostage in the Colombian jungle, thanks to a stunning July 2 helicopter rescue by state security forces, Ingrid Betancourt was canonized by the French media. And Saint Ingrid responded with inspiring grace and cool. She was feted at a glam-glitz reception by a rapturous Nicolas Sarkozy within hours of touching down in Paris on July 4. The fine features of the Paris-raised Colombian graced countless magazine covers, replacing the gaunt image that had been prevalent, one taken from a proof-of-life video and hung on the façades of city halls across France in solidarity. A *Paris Match* cover showed her laughing on a rooftop terrace in cashmere sweater and pearl earrings, with 40 pages inside about her "six years in Hell."

Hell it certainly was: Betancourt was chained for 12 hours a day to a tree, subjected to grueling 10-hour marches, ravaged by poisonous plants and insects and terrorized by ruthless guards. And those are just the details we know about. She admits that worse—

perhaps including sexual threats—remain concealed, probably until she writes her memoirs. In the meantime, she visited the Pope, received the Legion of Honor from Sarkozy at a Bastille Day ceremony and was described as worthy of a Nobel Peace Prize.

What's next for the former Colombian senator? She has said she does not know yet when she will return to Colombia or what her role will be. But she clearly has her eye on returning to Colombian politics. And her giant fame could reignite her prospects: about 31% of Colombians polled the day she was freed said they would vote for her for President. But first comes healing. In one of her first interviews, Betancourt was asked about her plans. She paused, then said, "Six days ago, I was chained to a tree ... I'm just trying to understand how I'm going to live from now on." —BY VIVENNE WALT

Betancourt was chained for 12 hours a day to a tree, subjected to grueling 10-hour marches ...

Robert Mugabe. Once a beacon of hope, a former prisoner of conscience has become a brutal dictator

THERE ARE FEW MORE STRIFE-TORN COUNTRIES THAN Zimbabwe under Robert Mugabe. Inflation has soared past 100,000%; as many as 8 in 10 are unemployed; and in the lead-up to a June 27 runoff election, Mugabe loyalists violently attacked opposition figures, while the 84-year-old President vowed that "only God" could remove him from power. He may be right: when he finally agreed to a power-sharing deal in September 2008, it kept him firmly in control of the military.

But it wasn't long ago that Mugabe was considered one of Africa's brightest postcolonial hopes. As recently as in 1994, Britain awarded him a knighthood. Mugabe was imprisoned from 1964 to 1975 for opposing white rule in the former British colony of Southern Rhodesia and later led its independence movement, becoming Prime Minister of the newly named Zimbabwe in 1980. In his first two years, he built schools, clinics and roads and promoted peace.

Yet, as he gained power, he grew intolerant of opposition. In the early 1980s, Mugabe's special forces massacred some 20,000 Ndebele tribespeople who supported a rival. He spent lavishly on houses, cars and military missions, sending thousands of troops to the Democratic Republic of Congo in 1998 for a costly anti-rebel campaign. In 2000 he encouraged the seizure of land from white farmers—a move that, combined with a drought, caused drastic food shortages.

Meanwhile, Mugabe painted himself as Africa's champion, calling Western nations "neocolonialists" striving to "keep us as slaves in our own country." Even as the U.N. condemned the political violence and the U.K. revoked his knighthood, Mugabe remained aloof. "He's not unaware of the fact that Zimbabwe's in chaos," said Robert Rotberg, director of the Program on Intrastate Conflict at Harvard's Kennedy School of Government. "He doesn't care." —BY TIFFANY SHARPLES

He vowed that "only God" could remove him from power

Tony Blair. Britain's former Prime Minister tackles two major challenges: the Middle East and global warming

WHEN MY FRIEND TONY BLAIR STEPPED DOWN AS U.K. Prime Minister in 2006, I advised him to take some time off with his family and make a list of the issues he felt passionately about and that he could continue to pursue. It was the least he had earned after a decade of modernizing his country's economy, making the U.K. one of the few nations to reduce their greenhouse-gas emissions more than required to meet their Kyoto target and leading the G-8 to historic commitments to support Africa and fight global poverty.

Tony listened to my advice graciously but ignored it completely by immediately accepting a new job as Middle East envoy for the Quartet [the U.S., Russia, E.U. and U.N]. I have always admired Tony's willingness to wade into troubled waters. Ten years ago, he did a masterly job in helping to end 30 years of sectarian violence and broker a lasting peace in Northern Ireland. Now he is demonstrating the same dedication and intensity to promoting economic opportunity in the Middle East, learning from his Irish experience that showing the concrete benefits of peace can play a crucial role in making a just and lasting peace possible.

Tony, 54, also knows that even the benefits of an en-during peace in the Middle East and the dramatic reductions in terrorism it would bring could be wiped away if we don't save the planet from the worst consequences of global warming. So he has taken on another big challenge: shaping a new global agreement to cut carbon emissions. Because my foundation is involved with projects to reduce greenhouse-gas emissions in more than 40 large cities on six continents, I know how important and difficult Tony's work is, and I look forward to the visionary leadership he will bring to it.

As his friend, I hope Tony finds fulfillment in advancing the public good as a private citizen. As a member of our interdependent global community, I thank him for not taking a day off when we need him the most.

—BY BILL CLINTON
Clinton, the 42nd U.S. President,
runs the William J. Clinton Foundation

Tony listened to my advice graciously but ignored it completely by immediately accepting a new job as Middle East envoy for the Quartet.

Muqtada al-Sadr. The fiery Shi'ite cleric remains a powerful force as a divided Iraq looks to the future

DURING 2003, U.S.-LED COALITION FORCES CONSID-ered Muqtada al-Sadr a renegade Shi'ite leader whose legitimacy was based mostly on the anti-Saddam Hussein legacies of his father and uncle. Although his Mahdi Army was small and loosely organized, he was able to quickly mobilize tens of thousands of Shi'ites from Baghdad to Basra.

In April 2004, al-Sadr's militia attacked coalition forces and took control of most provincial capitals in southern Iraq. In response, President Bush officially declared al-Sadr the enemy and ordered the military to capture or kill him. "We can't allow one man to change the course of the country," stated Bush in a video conference. "He must be wiped out." However, within a week, the White House reversed direction and ordered coalition forces to walk away from the mission. Negative media coverage was endangering the planned July 1, 2004, transfer of sovereignty to Iraq, which was heavily tied to Bush's re-election campaign.

That reversal was the turning point in al-Sadr's rise to power. It gave him legitimacy and enhanced his stature within the broader Iraqi community. The White House handed off this problem to the new Iraqi government with the clear understanding that he would not be arrest-ed but, rather, made a part of the political process. As a fierce opponent of what he calls "the American occupa-tion," al-Sadr, 34, appeals to the poor Shi'ite masses and thereby controls the stability of southern Iraq. By turning up the level of violence at will, he is able to control the coalition war-fighting environment, disrupt Iraq's political progress and affect American public opinion. Today, he is in a position to alter world events. He will inevitably continue as a major political power broker on the Iraq scene. But the die was cast in April 2004.

—BY RICARDO SANCHEZ
Lieut. General Sanchez commanded coalition forces in Iraq from June 2003 to June 2004

By turning up the level of violence at will, he is able to control the coalition war-fighting environment, disrupt Iraq's political progress and affect American public opinion.

Dispatches From Iraq

When the Bush Administration and U.S. generals launched a new strategy in Iraq in 2007—a surge that sent 30,000 additional troops to the occupied nation—many predicted the worst. Yet as two TIME dispatches from 2008 report, the surge has changed the situation in many ways, mostly for the better. Even so, the gains that have been made are fragile

Back to Baghdad
April 14, 2008

BY BOBBY GHOSH, FORMER BAGHDAD BUREAU CHIEF

WHEN I LEFT BAGHDAD LAST FALL AFTER SPENDING the best part of five years covering Iraq, I was far from sanguine about the surge; I had seen too many military plans promise much and deliver little. But by the end of the year 2007, Sunni insurgents I had known for years—men who had sworn blood oaths to fight the "occupier" until their dying breath—were joining forces with the Americans to fight al-Qaeda in Iraq. The vehemently anti-American Shi'ite cleric Muqtada al-Sadr had agreed to a cease-fire with the U.S. military, and his ill-disciplined militia, the Mahdi Army, seemed to be keeping its end of the bargain.

All these factors contributed to a steep drop in the frequency of insurgent attacks and suicide bombings, along with the rates of U.S. and Iraqi casualties. But remarkable as they are, the statistics don't tell you about the lives of ordinary Iraqis. So in mid-March, I returned for a two-week visit to get a firsthand feel for the changes. It seemed the perfect time to take soundings: the fifth anniversary of the start of the war and a little more than a year since the start of the surge.

The first sign of change comes when I board the Royal Jordanian Airlines flight from Amman. It's an Airbus A320, and that is good news. It means the flight will not end with the heart-stopping corkscrew landing that characterized all my previous arrivals in smaller, more nimble aircraft. If Royal Jordanian is willing to use a large jetliner, it can only mean that the likelihood of a missile attack has greatly diminished.

Driving into Baghdad from the airport, I see other changes. In commercial districts, more shops and businesses are open than there were a year ago. Shoppers are taking the time to haggle with vegetable vendors—a contrast to the furtive, hurried transactions I remember. There are no queues at the gas stations. Baghdad even sounds different. In my first two days, I hear no explosions or gunfire. At the TIME bureau in the Jadriyah district, we get four to six hours of electricity a day, up from just two hours. This means there are long spells

Baghdad even sounds different. In my first two days, I hear no explosions or gunfire.

Street scene *Iraqi women visit a market in Baghdad's Abu T'shir neighborhood in late January. Thanks to the success of the U.S. surge strategy, deaths of both Iraqis and Americans steeply declined in Baghdad and most areas of Iraq in 2008*

when you can hear the sounds of the city—traffic, the calls to prayer—instead of the constant roar of generators.

And the city looks different too. In our neighborhood, there are several new restaurants and kebab stands. Here and there, apartment buildings have received a fresh coat of paint. Even the concrete walls that crisscross much of Baghdad, erected by the U.S. military to protect neighborhoods from sectarian militias, have been prettified. The government has paid artists to paint huge, brightly colored murals on the walls, so a drive now takes you past bucolic scenes of farmers planting rice, fishermen in the marshes, peasants dancing in verdant valleys. The walls give Baghdad a somewhat disjointed feel, making it less a city than a series of contiguous fortresses.

Still, they have served their purpose. Within the walls, many Sunni neighborhoods that were once the focal points of sectarian violence are now policed by armed locals organized by the U.S. into Awakening Councils—or Sahwa, in Arabic. Many are former insurgents who are

happy to accept salaries ($300 per month, paid by the U.S., not the Iraqi government) from the men they once hoped to kill. They are nominally under American supervision but increasingly operate with a high degree of autonomy. The Sahwa are one part vigilante and two parts mafiosi, but like the walls, they too serve a purpose. In Sahwa-protected neighborhoods like al-Dora, Adhamiyah and Amariyah, sectarian killings are way down.

But perhaps the most remarkable change of all is in how Baghdadis view the U.S. military presence. A year ago, most Iraqis living outside the Green Zone saw the Americans as the main cause of their country's problems. Now, says Ali al-Dabbagh, spokesman for the government of Prime Minister Nouri al-Maliki, all the credit for the decline in violence is going to the U.S. military: "People think the Americans are like Superman, who can do anything."

While the Americans were coddling al-Sadr, the Prime Minister abruptly decided to confront him. Al-Maliki has been casting around for a military victory he could claim for his government rather than the U.S. military. On March 24, he made a surprise trip to the southern city of Basra and announced he was personally going to supervise an assault on the Mahdi Army, which vies with two other Shi'ite militias for supremacy there. It was the largest Iraqi military exercise since the fall of Saddam, involving 30,000 soldiers and policemen. The U.S. military, keen to showcase the growing competence of the Iraqi forces, allowed them to take the lead. Big mistake. The operation was a shambles. After a day's intense fighting, Iraqi commanders acknowledged that they had underestimated the strength of the Mahdi Army. With superior knowledge of Basra's backstreets and alleyways, the militias were able to outflank al-Maliki's forces. On March 26, the Prime Minister announced he was giving the militias 72 hours to disarm. Before the deadline expired, government representatives began negotiating a cease-fire with al-Sadr. Al-Maliki was left looking toothless and foolish; al-Sadr, stronger, more dangerous than ever.

For Sunnis, al-Sadr's continued clout is a warning and a provocation. In the district of Adhamiyah, a Sahwa fighter named Mahmoud tells me there can be no reconciliation between the sects "as long as Muqtada is alive." Then he makes a grim prediction: "Right now, the Americans want us to fight against al-Qaeda, and that's fine. But we know the real fight will be in the future, with the Mahdi Army. We are getting ready for it."

As I leave Baghdad, I reflect that for all the success of the surge, it has not exorcised Iraq's sectarian demons. Behind the painted walls, the murderous rage I saw in 2006 and '07 continues to fester. The Mahdi Army may have ceased fire, and Sunni insurgents may pose as friends of the U.S., but both are just waiting. Unless Americans have a major change of heart about maintaining a substantial and aggressive military presence in Iraq, all the gains of the past year will amount to nothing. ∎

In control *Shi'ite militants from radical cleric Muqtada al-Sadr's Mahdi Army strike a pose in Basra in late March*

When Will They Be Ready?
May 12, 2008

BY ABIGAIL HAUSLOHNER, TIME REPORTER, BAGHDAD

LIEUT. COLONEL WILLIAM ZEMP IS FULL OF PRAISE FOR the 700 Iraqi troops who have been helping bring peace to the countryside around Mahmudiya, a town 20 miles (30 km) south of Baghdad. As he leads his troops on patrol through a farming village, Zemp notes that less than six months ago, the area was prime insurgent territory and U.S. patrols routinely came under attack. On this April day, however, children poke their heads out of mud-brick doorways to wave, and two families even invite the troops to join in their modest midday meals. None of this would have been possible, Zemp says, without the efforts of the Iraqi army.

But where are the Iraqi troops that Zemp was hoping to bring along on this 7 a.m. sweep of the village? Stopping by the Iraqi base on the way to the patrol, Zemp finds that most of the Iraqi troops have not yet awakened. Zemp doesn't seem surprised or especially perturbed. "The [Iraqi] army is very good at what they do," he explains. "They just have a problem with sleeping in."

For months now, top U.S. military commanders have been trumpeting the growing strength of Iraq's 559,397-strong security forces, trained and armed by the U.S. military at a cost of $20.4 billion. But on the battlefield, the Iraqis are frequently found wanting and often have to be rescued by U.S. troops. A damning April 25 report by the Department of Defense's special inspector general for Iraq reconstruction says the Iraqi forces are still years away from being able to independently defend their country. Among other things, the report says, Iraqi security forces are still relying heavily on coalition forces for logistical support, and the shortage of officers "at all operational and tactical levels" is so severe that it could take a decade to address. Pentagon officials estimate that only two-thirds of Iraqi troops show up for duty at all.

This bodes ill for Iraq's security environment, which has deteriorated sharply since the start of the year. Many of the gains of the surge have already been lost; suicide attacks are up, and the rate of Iraqi and U.S. casualties has climbed. American troops, stretched to the limit, need the Iraqis to do more of the heavy lifting.

The inadequacy of Iraqi forces has come under a harsh spotlight since the March offensive in the southern city of Basra against Shi'ite militias loyal to the rebel cleric Muqtada al-Sadr. Barely a day into the offensive, al-Maliki had to call for backup as his troops ran into resistance from the militias. In disarray, some Iraqi troops refused to fight or surrendered; some switched sides and joined the militias. According to the Iraqi government, 1,300 soldiers deserted.

Southbound *Iraqi soldiers aboard a U.S. Air Force C-17 transport are being ferried to the southern city of Basra to join a March offensive against Shi'ite militants—a campaign that underscored the weakness of Iraq's army*

Top U.S. commanders continue to offer assurances that Iraqi forces are up to the challenge, emphasizing progress made over the recent setbacks. But soldiers working with Iraqi units on the ground say the praise is exaggerated. In Hilla, a dusty town south of Baghdad where a bloody battle raged in the streets at the end of March, some soldiers of the 4th Brigade Combat Team, 3rd Infantry Division, say their efforts were largely credited to an Iraqi force that did little. One soldier told TIME the Army had publicly commended the Iraqi troops for taking the lead in the battle. "But we did all the work," he said.

Not all Iraqi forces are so inept; several army brigades in the north, especially those composed of Kurds, have performed well on the battlefield. For the rest, the most charitable explanation is that it's unreasonable to expect a brand-new army and police force to stand up in such a short time. Iraqi soldiers get just six weeks' basic training, cops only eight—hardly the best preparation to do battle with a bewildering array of enemies, ranging from al-Qaeda terrorists and Iranian-backed Shi'ite militias to well-armed criminal gangs. Motivation is another problem: soldiers get starting salaries of $375 a month, policemen $95 a month. Iraqi commanders say that they are poorly equipped: they lack airpower and heavy weapons.

But there are also other, more worrisome reasons for the poor quality of Iraqi forces. Many American officers and soldiers say they don't trust their Iraqi counterparts. In the main, this is because Iraqi forces are rife with sectarian loyalties. Many soldiers and policemen were recruited from the very militias they are now being asked to kill or capture. American commanders would like to see more Sunnis in the Iraqi forces and are pressing al-Maliki to recruit more of the former insurgents to fight alongside U.S. troops; there are now some 90,000 such fighters, and their salaries, paid by the U.S., start at $300 a month. But the Iraqi government regards their loyalties as suspect and has dragged its feet in recruiting them.

Back in the village outside Mahmudiya, Zemp doesn't wait around for the Iraqi troops that are catching the extra z's. He continues with his patrol, bolstering his U.S. platoon with a handful of Iraqis in mismatched uniforms and a secondary commander. When the other members of the contingent arrive hours later, they march down the dirt path that has already been patrolled by U.S. troops, only to be called back and redirected. Their commander greets Zemp with a shrug. "I was sleeping," he says nonchalantly. For the U.S. military, however, the Iraqi battlefield performance in recent weeks should serve as a wakeup call. ∎

Russia Plays Rough

Moscow and Tbilisi stir up the ashes of the cold war

MADONNA GAVASHELI KNOWS WAR. SHE AND HER family were driven from their homes in South Ossetia 15 years ago in one of the many violent spasms that followed the breakup of the Soviet Union. They had just finished building a new brick house after years of careful saving when, in the first week of August, their village of Knolevi was pounded again as Russian jets screamed overhead and artillery erupted from the surrounding hills. Gavasheli, 29, cowered in the basement through the night, clinging to her two young children. At dawn they joined thousands of people heading for Tbilisi, Georgia's capital. When they arrived in the city hours later, they staggered into an abandoned kindergarten building with scores of other refugees.

Georgia and its border region of South Ossetia had squared off in an uneasy peace for more than a decade, since Moscow-leaning South Ossetia broke away from Georgia in the early 1990s, after the former Soviet republic gained its independence when the Soviet Union col-

lapsed. Ethnic Georgians are a minority in South Ossetia, 80% of whose citizens identify with North Ossetia across the border, which is part of Russia. After a protracted war that killed some 1,000 people and displaced thousands of ethnic Georgians from South Ossetia, Georgia was forced to sign a cease-fire agreement that left the territory—a tiny mountainous region a few football fields smaller than Rhode Island—effectively autonomous but unable to secure recognition by the international community.

Georgia's President, Mikhail Saakashvili, won election in 2004 by promising to recover the nation's breakaway territories and join NATO. So closely has he courted the U.S. that until war broke out with Russia, Georgia had 2,000 troops in Iraq, the third largest contingent after the U.S. and Britain. Meanwhile, Russia had provided financ-

Clamping down *Above, Georgian troops rush to defend Gori, the Georgian town closest to the border with South Ossetia, after a Russian bomb struck the apartment building at right*

GLEB GARANICH—REUTERS—LANDOV

ing, military protection and even passports to the South Ossetians, using their secession dreams, together with those of Abkhazia, another rebellious region of Georgia, as leverage against Tblisi's desire to join NATO.

Moscow sees Georgia's move toward NATO as part of a strategy of hostile encirclement of Russia by Western powers. When the Western alliance abetted Kosovo's secession from Serbia in February, and when NATO leaders agreed in April to consider accepting Ukraine and Georgia as members, Russia was further infuriated.

With the world's eyes turned to Beijing for the opening of the Olympic Games, Saakashvili moved first, and Russia pounced. The crisis began Aug. 7, after Georgia unleashed a massive artillery-and-rocket barrage on the South Ossetian capital of Tskhinvali and sent its military to reclaim control of the territory. Hours later, Russia launched its own offensive against Georgian forces.

A senior official at the U.S. State Department told TIME that Washington had grown alarmed by Saakashvili's misguided belief that his small country could take on the Russian military. Hours before Georgian tanks moved out, this official says he called Georgia's Foreign Minister, warning her that Russia was drawing Georgia into a trap, and urging her not to take the bait. No luck.

The result was a foregone conclusion. Three days after Georgia's tanks rolled into Tskhinvali, its forces retreated like a pack of wounded animals. Along the road to Tbilisi, military trucks sat abandoned with blown-out tires and shell-pocked panels. As some 35,000 South Ossetians fled, cars jammed the mountain passes leading out of the war zone. Thousands more scrambled out of Gori, the Georgian town closest to the South Ossetian border, where Georgian troops had gathered. Russian aerial attacks on Gori hit civilian targets, including an apartment building, killing about 60 people, according to the Georgian government.

Peace, of a sort, came on Aug. 12, when Russia agreed to a cease-fire and promised to begin withdrawing its troops, a process that continued for another week. But many

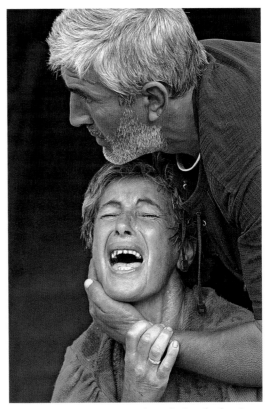

Anguish *A Georgian woman in Gori cries after hearing that her child had been killed in a nearby village*

Georgians were shocked that the U.S. did not do more to aid their cause, since Georgia is ostensibly a key Washington ally, giving rise to a furious sense of betrayal. "

In Tbilisi, a stunned Madonna Gavasheli told TIME her husband had vanished, along with their house. "There were many, many bombs," she said. "I do not even know how I got here." With tanks still rumbling along roads lined with ruins, and the region's future unclear, many Western leaders were wondering the same thing.

—BY VIVIENNE WALT

The Players. A tiny breakaway region of Georgia puts the U.S. and Russia at odds

1. Mikhail Saakashvili *Elected President of Georgia in 2004 after he helped lead the 2003 "rose revolution" that deposed Eduard Shevardnadze, he has aligned himself firmly with the U.S. as he squares off against Moscow.*

2. Vladimir Putin/George W. Bush *As Russian troops rolled into Georgia, Putin and Bush conferred at the opening of the Olympic Games in Beijing, left. Putin, who took the position of Prime Minister under Dmitri Medvedev when his two terms as President were over, quickly flew back to Russia, where he hurried to the war zone to direct Russian generals.*

3. Dmitri Medvedev *Putin's hand-picked successor put on a stern face during the crisis in Georgia, but events strongly suggested that only one man's words count in the Kremlin, and his first name is not Dmitri.*

Tinderbox? *The Sept. 20 bombing of the Marriott Hotel in Islamabad ratcheted up Pakistanis' sense of insecurity*

Entwined In Terror

Can Pakistan and Afghanistan suppress jihadist extremism?

PAKISTAN AND AFGHANISTAN ARE LIKE TWINS CONjoined," the President of the latter, Hamid Karzai, said in September, as he attended the inauguration of Asif Ali Zardari, the new President of the former. Karzai's reflection on the enduring woes of the neighboring nations was a fitting epitaph for 2008. After Pakistan was plunged into chaos by the December 2007 assassination of two-time former Prime Minister Benazir Bhutto and Karzai survived an assassination attempt, the two nations emerged as the new central front in the long war on jihadist terrorism. In Afghanistan, a resurgent Taliban showed its strength. But the year was especially rough in Pakistan, where Islamic extremism metastasized from the lawless tribal areas on the border with Afghanistan to

Pakistan's cities. By year's end, U.S. and Pakistani forces were openly sparring on the border between Afghanistan and Pakistan, as American troops sought al-Qaeda hiding places in Pakistan's forbidding Waziristan region.

Pakistan's plight became painfully apparent in the second half of the year. On Aug. 18, looking grim and sounding glum, President Pervez Musharraf announced his resignation on national TV, sparking celebrations among his people and anxiety in the U.S.: officials worried about the nation's stability, the security of its nuclear weapons, the intentions of its extremists and, not least, the country's enthusiasm for the global war on terrorism.

Two weeks later, terrorists tried (and failed) to assassinate Prime Minister Yousaf Raza Gilani in Islamabad.

Then, on Sept. 20, a bomber driving a truck packed with 1,300 lbs. of high-grade explosives rammed the front gate of the city's Marriott Hotel. The explosion destroyed the hotel, killed more than 50, injured hundreds and sent a powerful reminder to anyone who had not yet got the message: in some ways, Pakistan is beginning to resemble another nation in conflict—Iraq.

The picture in Afghanistan was, if anything, worse. According to a June 27 Pentagon report, Taliban militants there have regrouped after their fall from power and "coalesced into a resilient insurgency." That resilience, say Western military officials, has a lot to do with their ability to find sanctuary in Pakistan's lawless tribal areas along the border. CIA Director Michael Hayden has called the region an al-Qaeda "safe haven" that presents a "clear and present danger to Afghanistan, to Pakistan and to the West in general, and to the United States in particular."

A dramatic series of attacks by the Taliban underscored this point. On June 13, nine Americans were killed when Taliban fighters swarmed over a U.S. base in the eastern province of Kunar in the worst attack in three years. Three weeks later a mass assault on a jail freed hundreds of prisoners, and on July 7 a suicide bombing outside the Indian embassy killed 40 and injured more than 100. On Aug. 18 the Taliban attacked troops belonging to the International Security Assistance Force just 30 miles from the capital, Kabul, and 10 French soldiers died. The next day, militants launched a coordinated attack against one of the biggest U.S. bases in the country. As the violence mounted, Western troop casualties climbed: May and June exceeded the monthly death toll in Iraq.

Many of these assaults were planned and supported from safe havens across the border in the tribal areas of Pakistan. Frustrated by years of Pakistani inaction on this front, American forces stepped up their response: on Sept. 3 U.S. helicopters and ground troops crossed the border into Pakistan on a raid in which at least 17 Pakistanis were killed. Five days later, Predator drones launched Hellfire missiles on suspected al-Qaeda targets in Pakistani territory. When U.S. helicopters again ranged into Pakistan on Sept. 22, they were repelled by gunfire from Pakistani troops and local tribesmen.

The improvement of U.S. fortunes in Iraq, based on the troop surge, may provide some basis for optimism in Pakistan and Afghanistan. But perhaps the most discouraging part of comparing Kabul and Islamabad to Baghdad is the knowledge that things got much worse in Iraq before they got better. ∎

Close to home *A July 7 suicide bombing in Kabul that killed 40 people was the most brazen act of terrorism in Afghanistan's capital in recent years, underscoring the Taliban's expanded reach*

Asif Ali Zardari. Meet Pakistan's new boss, husband of the old boss

The final political act of Benazir Bhutto was revealed after her assassination: in her will, she handed leadership of the Pakistan People's Party (PPP) to her husband Asif Ali Zardari as if it were a family fief. Nine months later, he ascended to the presidency of this nation of 173 million people, the world's least stable nuclear power.

The son of a feudal landlord and cinema-house owner, Zardari wed Bhutto, Pakistan's political princess, in a 1987 arranged marriage, just as she entered politics. He took posts in her Cabinet and helped smooth the ruffled egos the sometimes haughty Bhutto left in her wake. He was also accused of being his wife's partner in corruption: the two were charged with laundering $1.5 billion through Swiss bank accounts. Zardari has spent 11 years in prison on charges including blackmail, corruption and conspiring to murder a political opponent who was also his wife's brother. He wriggled out of a 2006 corruption

trial in Britain by pleading mental instability.

This onetime playboy now has to balance U.S. demands for firm military action against the distrust of a public that largely blames the presence of foreign troops in Afghanistan for Pakistan's problems. To do so, he will have to convince Pakistanis that the war on terrorism is their war too.

Barriers to Peace

Hamas and Hizballah flex their muscles, and Israel marks time

"THIS IS A PROCESS THAT ALWAYS HAS TWO STEPS FOR-ward and one step back," President George W. Bush said in March about the decades-long quest to bro-ker a peace between Israel and the Palestinians. "We just need to make sure that it's just one step back." At that point, the most recent steps forward had been the Novem-ber 2007 Annapolis summit, at which both sides agreed upon a two-state solution for the first time, followed by Bush's first-ever state visit to Israel, in January 2008.

The inevitable one step backward came a few weeks af-ter Bush's trip, when Hamas militants unleashed chaos by blowing holes in a border wall separating the Gaza Strip from the Sinai Peninsula, which sent 350,000 Palestini-ans, who had been sequestered by an Israeli siege since the previous July, swarming into Egypt on a shopping spree.

Israel had corralled Gaza's 1.5 million people behind a 40-mile-long (64-km) concrete barrier in the hope that the blockade, which was tightened on Jan. 17 in response to rocket attacks from Gazan soil, would turn Palestinians against the Hamas ruling party. But by breaking the con-troversial quarantine (termed "collective punishment"

by many international aid organizations), Hamas earned the thanks of hungry Palestinians and gained a longer lease on power in Gaza. When Hamas celebrated this vic-tory by sending fresh barrages of rockets raining down on nearby Israeli towns, Israel retaliated with a five-day series of raids into Palestinian territory, killing at least 100 people.

Another small step forward came on June 19, when U.S. Secretary of State Condoleezza Rice brokered a cease-fire. Israel and Hamas agreed to end hostilities and discuss is-sues such as the reopening of Gaza's border crossings.

By that time, however, the focus of concern in the region had switched to Lebanon, where Hizballah—a Muslim ex-tremist group that, like Hamas, is bent on Israel's destruc-tion, but is far more powerful—gained a new stranglehold on the government. On May 8, Hizballah militiamen loyal to fire-breathing Sheik Hassan Nasrallah squared off against supporters of Prime Minister Fouad Siniora's

Breakout *In January, Palestinians who had been quarantined inside the Gaza Strip by an Israeli blockade cross into Egypt over remnants of a security barrier bombed by Hamas fighters*

Power play *Hizballah supporters in Beirut salute the prisoner exchange with Israel at an enormous July rally*

Olmert: Out. Facing challenges on every front, Israel gets a new leader. Will Tzipi Livni make a difference?

In a surprise July 30 announcement, Israel's Prime Minister, Ehud Olmert, said he would not seek re-election and would step down after his party's Sept. 17 leadership vote. At the time, Olmert was the subject of two separate criminal investigations over allegations of corruption; the unpopular PM had previously vowed to resign if charged.

Designated successor Tzipi Livni, 50, Israel's Foreign Affairs Minister, was born into an extremely nationalist family: both parents were fighters in the Irgun, the Jewish underground movement that fought the British in Palestine to create Israel. She served in the Israeli army and later joined Mossad, working for the intelligence service for several years in the early 1980s. She left the service to became a real estate lawyer before dipping into politics in 1999. Following her election to the Knesset, she became a protégée of Ariel Sharon's and gained a reputation for being modest and humorless; she's often referred to as "Israel's Mrs. Clean." Despite her early upbringing, Livni is seen as moderate on several issues, specifically the idea of a Palestinian state in the region.

U.S.-supported government in the capital, Beirut. After six hours of roiling street battles, the militants took control in areas of West Beirut that had previously been the government's preserve. This made for some incongruous scenes, as bearded men with rifles and rocket launchers secured lingerie shops and a Starbucks in the commercial Hamra district.

Hizballah's victory was hardly a surprise. Its Shi'ite militiamen, who number in the thousands and are armed by Syria and Iran, had emerged undefeated from their 2006 war with the mighty Israeli army, while Siniora's supporters were poorly armed amateurs on neighborhood patrol. Neither Lebanon's police nor the military—recipients of hundreds of millions of dollars in arms and training from the U.S.—dared to lift a finger against Hizballah. Despite the backing of the U.S., Western Europe and Arab states like Saudi Arabia, Siniora barely clung to power from his headquarters in the Grand Serail, a former Turkish fortress ringed by barbed wire and riot police.

This was all very bad news for Israel, and for the U.S. Behind Nasrallah and his Shi'ite fighters lurked a possibly greater threat: Iran. Hizballah's dominance in Beirut might allow Tehran to project its power into the Mediterranean Sea. And the militants' easy victory in the battle for Beirut left the U.S. yet again on the losing side of an Arab conflict, with little leverage and few options.

The picture in Lebanon grew grimmer in July, when Israel and Hizballah agreed to a deal in which Israel released several Lebanese terrorists, including militant icon Samir Kuntar, in exchange for the bodies of two Israeli soldiers, Eldad Regev and Ehud Goldwasser, whose capture in July 2006 triggered the month-long war between Israel and Hizballah. Nasrallah's party used the exchange as the occasion of a major celebration and show of power, flaunting its new control over Beirut's streets.

The spotlight returned to Israel in late July, when unpopular Prime Minister Ehud Olmert made the surprise announcement that he would step down after his party's September leadership vote. Many Israelis welcomed his departure, but the change also inevitably delayed progress on Israeli-Palestinian relations.

All these events came in a year when Israelis had hoped to be enjoying a national celebration commemorating the 60th anniversary of the nation's founding. But in the autumn, with diplomats in both Tel Aviv and Washington awaiting new leadership and possible new directions, the mood in Israel was more pensive than jubilant, and people on all sides of the peace process anxiously waited for the long-promised two steps forward. ■

Briefing

Ireland: "No!" *In a June 12 referendum, Irish voters cast their ballots against approving the European Union's (E.U.) Lisbon Treaty—the latest roadmap to what E.U. officials called a simpler, stronger, more transparent union—by a wide margin. The rebuff demonstrated that E.U. officials would have to do a better job of explaining the benefits they see in a closer union to average voters. Above, "Euroskeptics" support Ireland's decision at an E.U. meeting in Strasbourg, France, on June 18.*

The Leaderboard. Italy welcomes a new-old face, and in Cuba, Fidel finally steps down

Silvio Berlusconi *He's back! In April, voters dissatisfied with Italy's ongoing economic woes elected the billionaire media titan to lead them for the third time. He vowed to rescue the stalled Italian economy, resolve a garbage crisis and assist the faltering national airline, Alitalia. In October the flashy Berlusconi, 72, emerged at dawn from a Milan club and bragged "I only sleep three hours; the others are to make love."*

Raúl Castro *There was no surprise in Cuba on Feb. 24, when Parliament elected Raúl Castro, then 76, to succeed his ailing, 81-year-old brother Fidel, who resigned as President days before. Raúl, less charismatic and more pragmatic than his older brother, assured his people, "Fidel is irreplaceable." But he began instituting economic reforms, including leasing government land to private investors for the first time in decades.*

Hiding in plain sight *In the worst years of the Balkan wars of the 1990s, Bosnian Serb leader Radovan Karadzic, above left, led the anti-Muslim ethnic cleansing that peaked in the murder of some 8,000 people at Srebrenica in 1995. When the regime toppled, Karadzic lived on the run for over a decade—before he was arrested on July 21 in Belgrade. The trained psychiatrist's alter ego: Orthodox Christian alternative healer Dr. Dragan Dabic, right. Karadzic was extradited to the Netherlands to stand trial at a U.N. war crimes tribunal.*

Nuclear Scorecard

In September the International Atomic Energy Agency charged that Iran, while defying three sets of U.N. sanctions, had both stepped up the pace of uranium enrichment and slowed down compliance with demands to account for its secret nuclear research program. At top, a ballistic missile is paraded through Tehran's streets on Sept. 23.

In contrast, North Korea demolished the cooling tower above a reactor at Yongbyon in June, above, and the U.S. removed it from a list of states that sponsor terrorism in September. The nation's leader, Kim Jong Il, was reported to be very ill as this book went to press early in November.

Kashmir Boils Over—Again

Located between largely Hindu India and Muslim Pakistan, India's majority-Muslim state of Kashmir continues to be a hot spot. In August Indian police battled Muslims protesting the government's setting aside of land for a Hindu shrine in Srinagar and demanding freedom from India. More than 30 people died and hundreds were injured.

Dynamic Duo. France's President and his pop-star wife are on a roll

Plenty of pop albums have been ripped apart by music critics — including a few by model-singer turned French First Lady Carla Bruni, 40. But Bruni's 2008 effort, *Comme Si Rien N'Etait (As If Nothing Happened)*, released July 11, made her that rarest of things: a pop star savaged by critics *and* policy wonks. In one song, Bruni chose to liken her love for her husband Nicolas Sarkozy, 53, to addictive Colombian cocaine and Afghan heroin. *Sacre bleu!*

The controversy over Bruni's extragovernmental activities— and the fuss over her CD—was a virtual certainty, given the passions Sarkozy has unleashed with his reformist drive, polarizing style and long-established exploitation of his private life as part of his public relations mix.

In 2008 Sarkozy continued to insert himself into European and global affairs with a vigor long missing from French foreign policy. In a speech to both Houses of Parliament during a March visit to Britain, a pumped-up Sarkozy called for amity and coaxed a standing ovation out of British lawmakers old enough to remember decades of rivalry with the French. Sarkozy dominated France's welcome of freed hostage Isabel Betancourt in July; the next month he played a major role in the diplomacy that ended Russia's war with Georgia.

Society

Saline Solutions

American spas promoted mud baths in the 1940s, and the '70s brought in-home saunas and hot tubs. Now comes the next step in the quest for holistic relaxation: salt caves. East Europeans have long thought that sitting in naturally occurring salt caves could relieve allergies, asthma, eczema, hypertension, ulcers and stress. Recently, they've begun building simulated caves in the U.S. The Chicago area, thanks to its large Polish population, is the epicenter of the trend.

On an afternoon in 2008, 10 people reclined in deck chairs and on blankets under salty stalactites in Galos Caves, one such manmade cavern in Chicago. The recorded sound of waves filled the dimly lit room. It smelled like a seaside town. The floor, made of loose rock salt from the Dead Sea, was warmed to enhance the scent and coziness. After 45 minutes, for which they had paid $15 each, Dan Zegar, 50, and Denyse Waters, 57, told TIME's Jeninne Lee-St. John that they didn't want to leave. Waters thought the salt air had cleared her sinuses. Zegar's appreciation was broader: "If there are some medicinal properties to it, great. But it doesn't matter. It was so relaxing."

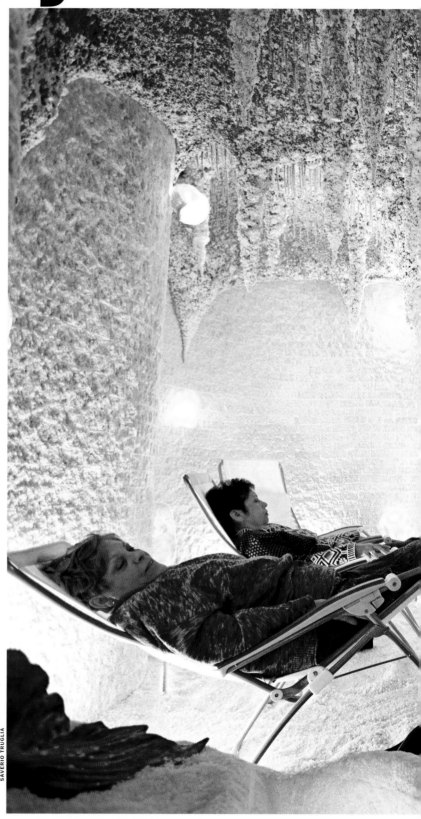

SAVERIO TRUGLIA

Randy Pausch. A dying, heroic professor, he gave life lessons, via YouTube, to millions of us

WHEN HIS PANCREATIC CANCER WAS DIAGNOSED in August 2006, doctors told Randy Pausch, 46, he had maybe a few months to live. He went through an aggressive course of treatment, surgery, chemotherapy; but a year later the disease had spread to his liver and spleen, and he was again told it was terminal. A popular computer-science professor at Carnegie Mellon University, Pausch delivered his "Last Lecture" on Sept. 18, 2007. It was a university tradition for popular professors to think hard about what mattered most to them and distill their ideas as though they had only one message left to give to the generation that followed. Pausch was the first for whom the exercise was literal.

Pausch's talk became a YouTube sensation, viewed many millions of times by people charmed by his easy manner; engaged by his lively insights into work, science and exploration; in awe of his complete lack of self-pity. He was the picture of health, with his thick dark hair and Muppet eyebrows, dropping to do push-ups on the stage, a defiant portrait of life with its edges all sharpened. Every sentence was soaked in gratitude, and listening to it could make you flinch at every time you'd whined or cheated or quit.

In October 2007 Pausch appeared on *Oprah*, and his audience widened. He testified before Congress for better cancer-research funding. He spent a day hanging out with the Pittsburgh Steelers, which he'd cited as his own childhood dream. In April 2008 his book, *The Last Lecture*, swooped high on the best-seller list. Three months later, on July 25, 2008, Paush died.

Wise men have said they're not scared of death, but they're a little scared of dying. Death is just a mystery; but dying is the journey we don't want to take, and Pausch used it to lead the living to a new place. It was as though he already knew more than he should, had dipped a ways into eternity and brought some pieces back for the rest of us to use in whatever ways and for whatever time we can. —BY NANCY GIBBS

It was as though he already ... had dipped a ways into eternity

Rick Warren. America's most prominent religious leader is ready to take on the world

I F RICK WARREN IS NOT QUITE TODAY'S BILLY GRAHAM, the revered evangelist who presided as "America's pastor" back when the U.S. affected a kind of Protestant civil religion, he is unquestionably the U.S.'s most influential and highest-profile churchman. The jovially hyperactive preacher, 54, is a natural leader, a pathological schmoozer, insatiably curious and often the smartest person in the room. Like Graham, he projects an authenticity that has helped him forge an exquisite set of political connections—in the White House, on both sides of the legislative aisle and abroad.

Warren is the author of one of the world's best-selling books, *The Purpose Driven Life*, and the founding pastor of one of the country's largest churches, the 23,000-member Saddleback Church in Lake Forest, Calif. On Aug. 16, he played the role of national inquisitor in a "civil forum" in which he civilly, serially, grilled presidential candidates John McCain and Barack Obama for an hour apiece. He is both leading and riding the newest wave of change in the evangelical community: an expansion beyond social conservatism to causes such as battling poverty, opposing torture and combatting global warming. A more cautious figure than Warren might have passed on the opportunity to become a political lightning rod. But he has spent the past few years positioning himself for just such a role as a suprapolitical, supracreedal arbiter of public virtues and religious responsibilities.

If Warren were content to be merely the most influential religious figure on the American political scene, that would be significant enough. He isn't. Five years ago, he concocted what he calls the PEACE plan, a bid to turn every single Christian church on earth into a provider of local health care, literacy and economic development, leadership training and spiritual growth. What drives Warren? He may not aspire to global mogulhood, but he is clearly near giddy over occupying a globetrotting-catalyst status normally reserved for ex-Presidents. —BY DAVID van BIEMA

The jovially hyperactive preacher is a natural leader, a pathological schmoozer, insatiably curious

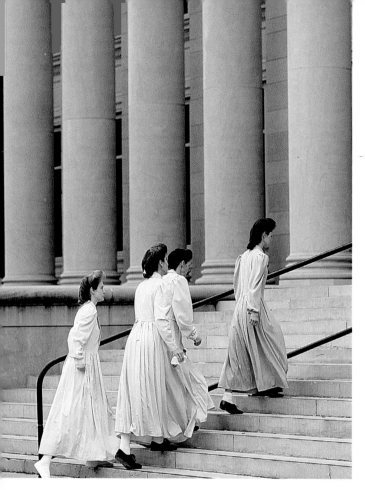

Mother and child disunion *At left,* FLDS *women enter a county courthouse in San Angelo, Texas. At right, authorities remove women and children from the sect's compound in Eldorado*

Sins of the Fathers

A raid on a polygamist sect in Texas highlights
tensions between religion and the law

O N APRIL 3, A CONVOY OF BLACK GOVERNMENT VE-
hicles converged on the Yearning for Zion Ranch,
an Eldorado, Texas, compound that houses a renegade Mormon sect, the Fundamentalist Church of Latter
Day Saints (FLDS). Summoned by a call to a child-abuse
hotline from a young girl who identified herself as "Sarah"
and said that she and other minors were in danger, state
officials removed 416 boys and girls from the ranch, more
than anyone had realized were living there. The raid on
the polygamist enclave produced haunting images: girls
in calico dresses, removed from log cabin houses, looking
questioningly into nowhere as they were led from their
homes into a secular world they have been taught to fear.
They sang hymns as they were driven away along with
139 adult women members of the sect.

The rest of the country was both appalled and fascinat-
ed, gawking at the sight of women seemingly dressed for
Little House on the Prairie, whose modest appearance was
jarringly at odds with their sexually aberrant lifestyle.
First came the jokes, then some hard realities sank in.

Hundreds of children were being separated from the only
families they knew. Shuttled from one temporary facility
to another, they were dispersed throughout Texas' over-
taxed foster-care system, from the Panhandle to Houston.

For weeks, investigators attempted to answer seemingly
basic questions—like the identities of the children, many
of whom gave different names and ages each time they
were interviewed—and tried to unravel the complex
maze of FLDS family relationships. While this frustrating
work proceeded, no charges were filed, and the only public details of the alleged child abuse centered on several
teenage mothers found at the ranch, who were described
in a request for a second search warrant.

The government called it a matter of child welfare; the
sect branded it religious persecution. Caught in the middle was Texas judge Barbara Walther, who was asked to
weigh requests from the parents to hold twice-daily
prayer meetings with the children and reunite nursing
mothers with the 77 kids who were under age 2. Prosecu-
tors worried that the prayer meetings might be used to in-

fluence the children "in a way to impede the ongoing investigation," but Walther's suggestion that mainstream Mormons might serve as neutral monitors was rejected by the official church, which asserts that the beliefs of the FLDS long ago diverged from Mormon orthodoxy. For the nursing mothers, the judge offered a lesson in contemporary feminism: "Every day in this country there are thousands of mothers who, after six weeks' maternity leave, must go back to work—and they deal with this issue."

Nor did the state of Texas seem to understand, entirely, what it was dealing with. At first glance, the Yearning for Zion Ranch has the look of other compounds built by apocalyptic cults led by charismatic tyrants. But this was a group with a tangled history many generations deep. Members of such renegade polygamous sects have intermarried and interbred to the point that, in the words of writer Jon Krakauer, their "relationships are almost impossible to make sense of without a flowchart."

In 1953, Arizona authorities had moved against an FLDS community, trying to root out the fathers and remove the children. But after a couple of years of costly court cases and a tide of public opinion in favor of keeping families together—no matter how unconventional—authorities chose to look away. The Eldorado families resorted to similar tactics this time, creating websites rich with photographs of tearful mothers, menacing deputies and frightened kids. Some of the sect's mothers appeared on *Larry King Live*, pleading for the return of their children.

Members of the FLDS are followers of imprisoned leader Warren Jeffs, convicted in 2007 in Utah of being an accomplice to rape after he used his authority as "Prophet" to force a 14-year-old girl to marry. Evidence gathered during the 2008 raid included two photos of young girls—one age 12, the other 13—sitting in Jeffs' lap and embracing him, and kissing him in one photo. One was marked "first anniversary," the other as a marriage photo.

By May, investigators came to the embarrassing conclusion that the call that triggered the raid was apparently a hoax: "Sarah" was actually an adult woman living in Colorado who had a history of impersonating victims of abuse. As criticism mounted, civil libertarians began to question whether, absent a specific complaint, government officials had the authority to separate children from their families merely because they might be at risk of abuse in the future. On May 29, the Texas Supreme Court answered this question by ordering the state's child welfare authorities to return all the children to their parents.

The battle isn't over: Texas officials continue to probe the sect's labyrinthine relationships. As of September 2008, nine FLDS members, including Jeffs, have been indicted on charges of sexual assault of children and bigamy.

—BY DAVID VON DREHLE AND HILARY HYLTON

A world apart *State vehicles park at the Yearning for Zion Ranch during the April 8 raid*

Heartthrobs of The Year *The hottest boy band in the land in 2008 was the Jonas Brothers. From left, that's Nick, 16, Joe, 19, and Kevin, 21, for those who are not among the target audience.*

Groomed by the famously regimented Disney marketing machine, the brothers released their third album in 2008, A Little Bit Longer. *Said* TIME's *Josh Tyrangiel: "Three adorable haircuts related by birth and a willingness to appear on any talk show that will have them."*

Paparazzi Bait. Two sets of twins and a trio of brothers are among those stalked by Gawker in 2008

Divorce Settlement of the Year

"I'm so happy with this," said Heather Mills, 40, after being awarded $49 million by a London judge as a settlement in the trial for divorce initiated by Paul McCartney, 65. She was perhaps less enthused over comments made by the judge in the case, Justice Hugh Bennett, who noted in a 58-page document issued after the trial—which she unsuccessfully sought to suppress—that "the husband's evidence was, in my judgment, balanced. He expressed himself moderately, though at times with justifiable irritation, if not anger. He was consistent, accurate and honest." Of Mills' testimony, however, Bennett wrote, "Much of her evidence, both written and oral, was not just inconsistent and inaccurate, but also less than candid."

Power Parents of the Year

TIME named actors Brad Pitt, 44, and Angelina Jolie, 32, to the TIME 100 in 2008 but classified them as Heroes & Inspirations rather than Entertainers. As contributor George Clooney noted, they have served as U.S. goodwill ambassadors abroad, bringing help to Pakistan after the 2005 earthquake and more recently focusing awareness on the victims of atrocities in Darfur.

In the U.S., the couple is running a project to finance and build 150 new homes in New Orleans' Ninth Ward. And speaking of home, on July 12 Jolie gave birth to twins Knox Leon and Vivienne Marcheline, who joined the pair's extended brood of four other kids.

Weddings of the Year

His last year in office didn't offer many joys to George W. Bush, who found himself approaching record-low approval ratings. But the Bush family enjoyed a respite from politics on May 10, when daughter Jenna, 26, at right above, married M.B.A. student Henry C. Hager, left. That's First Twin Barbara on the left in the family portrait.

The year's most notable same-sex marriage: TV host Ellen DeGeneres, 50, and Australian actor Portia de Rossi, 35, top right, wed on Aug. 16 at their Beverly Hills home after California's Supreme Court ruled gay marriage legal.

Photo op of the year *"I think it's really arty. It wasn't [done] in a skanky way." Thus did America's big sister, Miley Cyrus, describe a* Vanity Fair *image of herself, tousled and bare, by celebrity photographer Annie Liebovitz . Many parents of fans of Disney Channel's hit* Hannah Montana, *on the other hand, saw not an homage to classical portraiture but a topless 15-year-old. Cyrus later apologized for the photos, taken with the blessing of her manager mother and* Hannah *co-star father, Billy Ray Cyrus.*

Birthdays of the Year. A trio of ageless stars celebrates big birthdays—but who's counting?

1. Madonna, 50 *The Material Girl celebrated her half-century and a new 10-year $120 million deal with entertainment giant Live Nation by taking songs from her* Hard Candy *album on the road in the Sticky & Sweet tour, her latest visual extravaganza. In October she and her British husband, film director Guy Ritchie, announced they would divorce after a marriage that lasted eight years.*

2. Michael Jackson, 50 *The Gloved One remained far from the limelight as he turned 50 ("His nose turned 14," observed* TIME's *Pop Chart page). But he did offer fans a re-release of* Thriller *to mark the 25th anniversary of the pop masterpiece, featuring new vocals by Akon, Fergie and will.i.am.* TIME *critic Richard Corliss's verdict: "The singing is imitative, the remixing hasty and dull." Ouch.*

3. Mick Jagger, 65 *The Rolling Stones frontman is still resting up from the two-year Bigger Bang tour, which yielded the well-reviewed 2008 Martin Scorsese film* Shine a Light. *Sir Mick is now eligible for a British pension of £91 a week.*

Briefing

Pilgrim *Pope Benedict XVI paid his first visit to his American flock in April, beginning in Washington and ending in New York City five days later. Above, the Pontiff, 81, visits Yankee Stadium to say Mass. The Pope, observed* TIME's *David van Biema, "has a soft spot for Americans. [He] knows that religious conflict may be the 21st century's great challenge. He also appears to sense that American power alone won't solve it—but that the power of American values still might."*

Gay Marriage: More Controversy

Below, San Francisco Mayor Gavin Newsom presides over the vows of longtime gay activists Del Martin, 87, left, and partner Phyllis Lyon, 84, after California's Supreme Court ruled that gay marriages are legal. In October Connecticut's Supreme Court also ruled the unions were legal, but the issue remains controversial. In the November general election Californians approved by a narrow margin an amendment that will make gay marriage constitutionally invalid.

Circular logic *You say you want a revolution? Traffic signs like the one above are becoming more familiar to Americans, as the number of roundabouts is booming in the U.S. About 1,000 of them have been built in 25 states, and research bears out the benefits of the circular intersections: they produce a steep drop in accidents involving injuries, save surprisingly large amounts of gas per circle, reduce delays—and they are cheaper to build.*

The Pursuit of Purity

Critics have called them odd, creepy and oppressive, but purity balls are booming in the U.S., as parents opposed to a culture they feel promotes moral laxity hold father-daughter events to support moral values. At the affairs, fathers vow to practice fidelity, shun pornography and guide daughters amid a "culture of chaos," while teen girls vow to remain sexually abstinent until marriage. The Abstinence Clearinghouse reports that 4,000 purity balls were held in the U.S. in 2007, and the number is growing.

This Bud's for Belgium

Anheuser-Busch may not have the ring of an all-American name, but Budweiser and the brewer's other suds account for nearly half of all U.S. beer sales. With its team of Clydesdale horses and flashy Super Bowl ads, the St. Louis–based brewer is a national institution. So when giant Belgian brewer InBev, maker of Stella Artois, launched a bid to acquire its U.S. rival, CEO August Busch IV scrambled to hold it off. But InBev's pockets were deeper: on July 13, Anheuser-Busch accepted the offer, making InBev the world's largest brewer.

Back to The Grind

For Starbucks mogul Howard Schultz, 2008 was a year to wake up and sell the coffee. Schultz took over the company in 1987 and grew it from a six-shop seller of beans into a coffee colossus with $10 billion in yearly sales and 16,000 stores in 44 nations. But Starbucks' star has lately stopped rising: traffic at U.S. stores dropped for the first time in history, comparable-store sales turned negative, and its stock hit the skids.

Facing complaints that in its pursuit of growth the company strayed too far from its roots, Schultz, who had ceded his CEO position for a place on the board in 2000, again became CEO in January. He quickly began closing underperforming stores and slowing down openings. "It's an adventure," Schultz told TIME.

Since You Asked ...

Rachael Ray. TV's perky cook replies to our readers' queries

If you were stranded on an island but miraculously it had a refrigerator, what 10 ingredients could you absolutely not do without?

Matthew LeMay, PHILADELPHIA

I'd have to have olive oil, garlic, pasta, canned fish—anchovies, if I had to pick just one—cheese. If my husband were on the island with me, then I have to have salami. I've got to have some prosecco and some other wine, and you need your roughage, so escarole—and I have to have some beans, so I'd pick white.

What were your favorite foods as a child?

Soyeun Yang, SUPERIOR, COLO.

My grandfather lived with us and was my caretaker, so I liked everything that old Italian men liked. I liked sardines and squid and eating calamari with your fingers and anything with anchovies, anything with garlic and oil. I still eat much the same way today. I was not a very popular girl when I opened my lunch sack.

What is your favorite fast food?

Andy S. White, SCHODACK, N.Y.

There isn't a fast food that I don't like, really. *[Laughs.]*

Sport

DOUG PENSINGER—GETTY IMAGES

And the Winner Is ...

Can you spot the man who just lost the biggest golf tournament of his life? That would be the jolly gentleman on the left, Rocco Mediate. First Mediate had to watch perennial champ Tiger Woods pull off a series of cliff-hanger putts to force a one-day playoff with him in the 2008 U.S. Open tournament at the Torrey Pines course outside San Diego. Then Mediate had to endure another magical Woods comeback to force the playoff duel into an immediate, first-winner-of-a-hole-takes-all, sudden-death round. And at last, it was Mediate who flinched: Woods won the very first hole—and the tournament.

But no trash-talk and no frowns here. After the Monday playoff—which kept even Americans who don't know a driver from a sand wedge glued to TV sets in a million workplaces across the land—the friendly foes vied to outdo each other one more time: with compliments. "Nothing he does surprises me," said Mediate of Woods. "People don't realize how much of a competitor he is," said Woods of Mediate.

And that's why there really wasn't a loser in this year's Open. As TIME's Michael Elliott observed, "There can be no golf player or fan ... who did not watch the tussle between Tiger Woods and Rocco Mediate ... and think, To hell with bragging rights, this is *amazing.*"

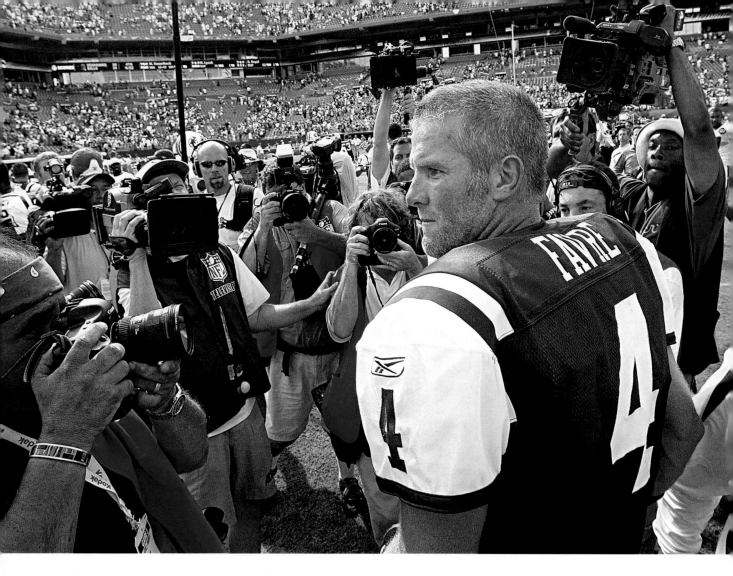

Brett Favre. He said goodbye, then thought twice, joining other champions who couldn't call it quits

SO MUCH FOR GOING GENTLY INTO THAT GOOD night. Four months after a tearful press conference that left an entire state of Cheeseheads in mourning, storied Green Bay Packers quarterback Brett Favre announced he wanted to return from retirement. The only problem: the Packers were ready to wrap up his legacy, even if he wasn't. After several weeks of melodrama, Favre ended up sporting the unlikely colors of green and white, as the new quarterback of the New York Jets.

Favre, 38, is far from the first athlete to flip-flop on bidding farewell to his game. Pitcher Roger Clemens, the king of comebacks, has retired three times now. Lance Armstrong left cycling in 1996 to battle cancer, returned to win seven consecutive Tour de France titles, then retired again. In September 2008, he said he would begin training to compete in the 2009 Tour de France. Other stars have re-emerged to save a struggling franchise, like Michael Jordan, who proclaimed his 1995 return to the Chicago Bulls after a failed bid at pro baseball with a two-word press release: "I'm back."

The deathless *Rocky* series aside, the "sweet science"

specializes in sequels: Muhammad Ali re-entered the ring three years after the New York State Boxing Commission revoked his license for refusing to serve in Vietnam, while George Foreman, who quit boxing in 1974, became the oldest fighter to win a major heavyweight title 20 years later. It's not just athletes: in 2006, Barbra Streisand fans nearly took their idol to court when the singer announced a series of farewell shows—seven years after her last "last-ever" tour.

Blame the homecomings on boredom, nostalgia or an indomitable drive to compete ("I got the itch," Favre reportedly told Packers teammate Al Harris). But not all comebacks are success stories. Just ask Bjorn Borg, who left tennis in 1983 and unretired eight years later, in 1991, wooden racquet in hand. He didn't win a single match that year. —BY M.J. STEPHEY

The only problem: the Packers were ready to wrap up Favre's legacy, even if he wasn't

Padraig Harrington. The Irish charmer perfects his winning ways—with fans and on the course

I N THE MIDDLE OF THE FAIRWAY OF THE FINAL HOLE OF the British Open golf championship, in one of the sport's most tense moments, Padraig Harrington's caddy broke the golfer's routine with an interjection. "Happy?" he asked. Harrington was majestically unfazed. "Yep," the Irish pro shot back before firing off an iron shot that soared to within 15 feet of the hole and sealed his victory.

The 137th Open Championship, held at Royal Birkdale near Liverpool in July, was not supposed to be a joyous affair. Going into the final day's play, in fact, all signs suggested a narrative of torment, inner demons and redemption in the clutches of the body's inexorable decline. That was all taking place in the livin'-large form of 53-year-old third-round leader Greg Norman. But on the final day, the Australian thrashed and grimaced his way to yet another near miss at a major championship. Instead, it was a chap named Paddy, with a big grin and sparkling eyes, who stole the show. Fusing newfound sunny implacability to his flawless technique, Harrington dominated the pro tour in the absence of Tiger Woods, going on to win the year's final major, the PGA Championship, at Michigan's Oakland Hills Country Club.

Ironically, Harrington has earned this mental strength through a tale of redemption. His plodding, mulish gait and mechanical style led many to label him a "journeyman" even before his 30th birthday, and for many years he was a consistent nearly-man, just like Norman. Between his first professional victory, in 1998, and his second two years later, he recorded nine runner-up finishes. In his joyous acceptance speech at the Open, Harrington recounted a telling anecdote from his second round. After a double bogey that could have taken him out of the running, a fan reached over the ropes, patted him on the shoulder and said, "Don't worry about it, Paddy. On Monday I have to go back to being a plumber." —BY EBEN HARREL

For many years he was a consistent nearly-man, just like Greg Norman

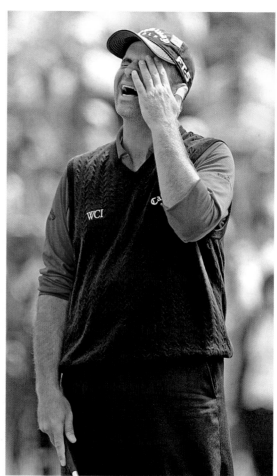

Two for the Show

Forget Obama/McCain: sports fans thrilled to a quartet of riveting duels in 2008 that will be remembered for years

U.S. Open: Tiger Woods vs. Rocco Mediate

FOLLOWERS OF PRO GOLF KNOW AND LOVE Rocco Mediate, 45, as a happy warrior who is often in contention in tournaments but has battled back problems, uncomplainingly, for years and has never been a star. As for Tiger Woods: you don't have to follow golf at all to know that, at 32, he may be the greatest player in history. When the likable veteran and the dazzling champ tangled at the 2008 U.S. Open at the Torrey Pines course outside San Diego, their clash produced one of the most exciting Opens in memory.

Mediate scrambled just to compete: ranked No. 158 in the world, he was forced to win a place in the Open in a qualifying match. As for No. 1, Woods was nursing a knee injury so

serious that doctors urged him to withdraw. But he kept mum about the ailment and thrilled fans by making a series of clutch shots, including a must-do putt on the 18th green on Sunday, to tie the surprising Mediate at the end of 72 holes. In Monday's playoff, Woods once again was forced to sink a putt on 18 to tie Mediate. Done. Now it was on to sudden death, and on the first hole Woods prevailed, notching a par to Mediate's bogey, after which the two men shared a hug.

Said Woods: "You play through it and suck it up and get it done." Said Mediate: "The guy's impossible to beat." Any questions?

■ **WINNER: WOODS**

Playing through
Above, Woods sinks a key putt on the 72nd hole to tie Mediate, who on the right is seen reacting after missing a putt on the fifth hole of the playoff round. After winning, Woods said he would undergo knee surgery and miss the rest of the year's events

Wimbledon: Serena Williams vs. Venus Williams

FOR MORE THAN A DECADE NOW, THE WILLIAMS sisters, Venus and Serena, have battled each other in one of the greatest sibling rivalries in the history of sport. Going into 2008, the two had faced off for one of tennis' four major titles six times, and younger sister Serena had won five of them. She snagged two of those wins at the game's premier event, the Wimbledon tourney, in 2002 and '03.

Yet if the sisters are rivals on the court, they are so close that they shared an apartment at this year's Wimbledon tournament, and they team up as a formidable doubles pair. The 2003 death of their older half sister, Yetunde Price, appears to have made them closer than ever, even as it seemed to trigger a decline in the quality of their play. In 2008 they proved that they are back in top form: indeed, their '08 Wimbledon showdown was their first meeting in a Grand Slam final in five years.

It was worth the wait. Serena jumped to an early lead, up 4-2 in the first set. But on a gusty day at Centre Court, Venus fought back to win in two sets, 7-5, 6-4. At one point she smashed a 129-m.p.h. serve—tying her own women's record—and she consistently won the longer rallies. The victory gave Venus her fifth singles title at Wimbledon, almost matching Serena's total of major titles; Venus had now won seven to Serena's eight.

Two hours later the sisters took the same side of the court, teaming up to win their third women's doubles title at Wimbledon. A month later they took another doubles gold medal at the Beijing Olympics. But at the U.S. Open in New York City, Serena exacted her revenge: she beat Venus in the quarterfinals on the way to winning the tournament. Time to revise that running total of major titles: it's now 9-7, Serena. But, hey, Who's counting?

■ **WINNER: VENUS WILLIAMS**

A tale of two sisters *Age 26 at Wimbledon, Serena, left, is the younger sister; Venus is 28. Said Venus: "I'll give her the scouting report every time [on other players]. I just won't give her tips on how to beat me"*

NBA Finals: Boston Celtics
vs. Los Angeles Lakers

AFTER YEARS OF LETHARGIC FINALS MATCH-UPS (SPURS-Nets! Spurs-Pistons! Anything with the Spurs!), basketball fans finally got lucky in 2008: the NBA finals featured the Los Angeles Lakers and Boston Celtics in a rekindling of the sport's most thrilling rivalry. The much anticipated match-up—the 11th time the teams had played for the championship—was touted with endless clips of Bill Russell, Jerry West, Elgin Baylor and, of course, Bird vs. Magic. And the '08 storyline was promising. The latest battle between the NBA's two most storied franchises featured the sport's most breathtaking player, the Lakers' Kobe Bryant, against Boston's vaunted Big Three: Kevin Garnett, Paul Pierce and Ray Allen, the trinity that had six-handedly redeemed the stirring Celtics tradition of greatness.

In 2007 the Celtics, one of the most celebrated sport franchises, winners of 16 titles, were the joke of the NBA. They finished 24-58 and at one point doormatted 18 straight games. During the off-season, Celtics GM Danny Ainge pulled off a pair of heists, bringing Garnett, the 6-ft. 11-in. ex-MVP who is one of the most versatile players ever, and sweet-shooting guard Allen to Boston. There they joined Pierce, an automatic scorer and a six-time All-Star himself. The trio clicked. Result: Boston's record was a stunning 66-16 in the regular season.

Return to glory *Above, Paul Pierce, the six-time All-Star who has led a long-suffering Celtics squad, holds the NBA trophy after Boston won the title on their home court. He was named MVP of the championship series. Kobe Bryant (24), Lamar Odom (7) and the other Lakers couldn't match the intensity of the revitalized Celtics in the finals*

Even so, no one wanted a Boston Massacre in the finals. But that's what they got: Boston swept the first two games at home, made a thrilling comeback to steal one of the three games in Los Angeles, then smothered the Lakers in the sixth game in Boston, winning 131-92 to claim the title. The finals fizzled, but the redemption of the Celtics and of a storied rivalry made 2008 a standout year in recent NBA history.

■ **WINNER: CELTICS**

Wimbledon: Rafael Nadal vs. Roger Federer

HOW GOOD WAS THE 2008 MEN'S SINGLES final at Wimbledon? According to SPORTS ILLUSTRATED, "Let's be unequivocal: it was the greatest match ever played." John McEnroe agreed—and so did the man in the best position to know, Rafael Nadal. The swashbuckling Spaniard's triumph over the elegant Swiss, Roger Federer, came after 4 hr. 48 min. of a rain-interrupted match that ended at 9:15 p.m. in gloom so deep that both players said they could barely see the ball.

For more than three years, Nadal and Federer had dueled atop the men's game. Nadal first emerged as a clay-court expert, and he had beaten Federer three straight times to win the game's only major on clay, the French Open, including a rout in the 2008 match. But he had never beaten Federer on Wimbledon's grass courts, where the Swiss had won five straight times and was gunning for No. 6 in 2008. Going into Wimbledon, Federer had been No. 1 for a record 231 consecutive weeks; Nadal had been No. 2 for a record 154 weeks. Now that's a rivalry.

In the epic, seesaw final, Federer fought back from two sets behind, drawing even after Nadal wasted two match points in a fourth-set tiebreaker. Nadal then survived two Federer match points at 5-4 in the fifth set, before winning 9-7. "In the last game, I didn't see nothing," said Nadal of the gloom. Except history, perhaps.

■ **WINNER: NADAL**

Upset *The fiery Nadal, 22, lagged behind the cool Federer, 27, for years, unable to beat him on grass or composition courts. "Rafa's a deserving champion," said Federer after Wimbledon. The Swiss returned to form in September, beating Andy Murray to win his fifth U.S. Open. But Nadal won the gold medal at the Beijing Olympics and held on to his new ranking as the No. 1 men's player*

Briefing

Big Brown's bad break *First he cruised to a 4¾-length win in the Kentucky Derby, above. Then Big Brown, a Kentucky-bred descendant of Native Dancer, so overpowered the Preakness field that jockey Ken Desormeaux eased him across the finish. Would the big guy become the first Triple Crown winner since Affirmed in 1978? No: a crack was discovered in his hoof after the Preakness, and Big Brown finished ninth and last at the Belmont Stakes. In October, the fleet colt was forced to retire.*

Philadelphia Story: Series Rings at Last

Baseball's Year of the Underdog found two unexpected but fine teams facing off in the World Series: Tampa Bay's young Rays and Philadelphia's long-suffering Phillies. The Rays had momentum on their side, sporting a Cinderella story, Mohawk haircuts and a triumph in the playoffs over Boston's tough Red Sox. But the slugging Phils dominated, winning their first Series since 1980 by a 4-1 margin. The last game was cut short in the 6th inning by rain; it was two nights later when catcher Carlos Ruiz and pitcher Brad Lidge hugged in victory, below.

Blade runner *Born without major bones in his legs and feet, South Africa's Oscar Pistorius lost his lower limbs to amputation before he was a year old. Yet as he grew up, so did the science of prosthetics; he now runs on carbon-fiber blades known as Cheetahs. After winning gold in the 200 m at the Athens Paralympics in 2004, Pistorius hoped to compete in the Beijing Olympics. A battle between track's regulating bodies as to whether the blades gave him an unfair boost left him eligible for the Games, but he just missed qualifying. His revenge: gold medals in the 100-, 200- and 400-m events in the Beijing Paralympics.*

The Brady Bunch, sans Brady

He's taken the New England Patriots to four Super Bowls and won three of them. He has also won countless awards, has hosted *Saturday Night Live* and dates Brazilian model Gisele Bündchen. But even ace quarterback Tom Brady isn't quite invincible. In the Pats' first game of the 2008 season, Brady took a hard hit from Kansas City Chiefs safety Bernard Pollard, below, and required knee surgery that will sideline him until fall 2009. The Patriots' record without their leader: not good enough to Bowl anyone over.

The People's Choice

It was a victory for underdogs everywhere. At the 132nd Westminster Kennel Club Dog Show in New York City, tuxedoed judges bearing shiny trophies descended on Uno, the merry little beagle that became the first of his kind to win Best in Show, ever. The sold-out crowd in Madison Square Garden cheered from the moment Uno first appeared, and the judges paid heed: the beagle, if lowly, has ranked among the top 10 most popular breeds in the U.S. for nearly a century. Uno's first reward: steak on a silver platter at Sardi's.

Back in The Saddle Again

Cyclist Lance Armstrong has been one of the most popular athletes in the U.S. in the past decade, and his record of seven straight wins in his sport's biggest event, the Tour de France, is likely to stand for decades to come. Part of Armstrong's appeal is the courage he displayed in overcoming the testicular cancer that struck when he was 25, and since his retirement from racing in 2005, he has devoted much of this time to his Live Strong foundation, which supports cancer research.

On Sept. 9, Armstrong, 37 in 2008, surprised sports fans by declaring he would return to cycling in 2009 and hoped to compete in a few major races, including the Tour de France. One reason: to raise worldwide awareness of the dangers of cancer. Another: to prove once and for all that he races clean, for he is still fighting rumors that some of his Tour victories were drug-enhanced.

Since You Asked ...

John Madden. The NFL's legendary coach and broadcaster replies to our readers' queries

Do you think professional football players should be considered role models?

Owen Murphy, PHILADELPHIA

Yes, I do, and I think it ought to even be written in their contracts. I don't think they have the right to say they are or they're not, because they are, and they ought to accept that.

What do you think are some traits of leadership?

Lee Reese, TAMPA, FLA.

Just being a hard worker and a good player. Some people think that it's about talking. If a guy doesn't work hard and doesn't play well, he can't lead anything. All he is, is a talker.

What would you say is the biggest difference between the game when you coached and football today?

Nate Barton, RALEIGH, N.C.

We used to play the same guys on offense and defense just about every down. Now they have these packages—every down, five or six guys come in on offense or defense. Every play, you have to locate who's in the game and what they're doing.

Olympics '08

The Rockets' Red Glare

The Beijing Olympics offered a study in irony, as host nation China—buoyant with the riches of newly unleashed capitalism—orchestrated the Games as a showcase to declare its arrival on the world stage as a great power. Yet the splash and spectacle were served up by a one-party government that strove to keep all signs of protest or free speech out of public view during the Games.

At right, fireworks paint the sky around the futuristic National Stadium, or "Bird's Nest," designed by Swiss firm Herzog & de Meuron, during the opening ceremonies. At lower right is the equally exuberant Beijing National Aquatics Center, dubbed the "Water Cube," site of the swimming and diving events. Designed by Australian firm PTW, its exterior was based on the physics of soap bubbles. Yet these innovative structures were surrounded at all times by a picket line of soldiers who kept a rigid grip on Beijing's well-scrubbed streets.

GAMMA—EYEDEA—ZUMA PRESS

The splash and spectacle were served up by a one-party government that strove to keep all signs of protest or free speech out of public view

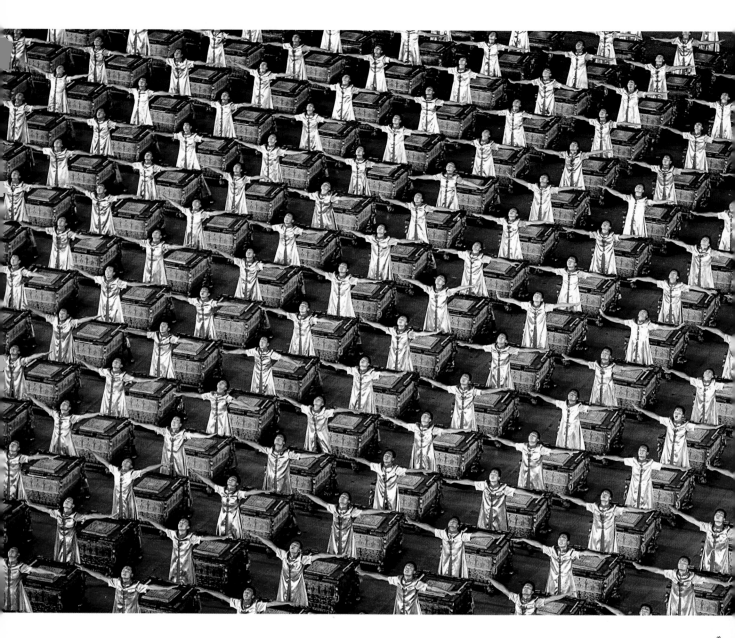

Barnum in Beijing *The opening ceremonies of the Beijing Games were staged by Chinese film director Zhang Yimou, known for* Raise the Red Lantern, Hero *and* House of Flying Daggers, *movies saturated in color and pageantry. Harking back to the days of Cecil B. DeMille, he oversaw a production that was colossal in every way: A cast of thousands! Gravity-defying wire-work! Dancers lit up like fireflies! Fireworks forming footprints in the sky! Drawing on the Chinese mastery of rigorously synchronized multiplicity, the spectacle was thrilling indeed, and blessedly free of much, if not all, of the kitsch associated with past Olympic openings. Above, massed drummers take a bow.*

Going global *Acrobats on wires ramble across an illuminated globe during the opening ceremonies, which were staged on a most fortuitous date in China, where the number 8 is regarded as good luck: 8/8/08. After the ceremony, some of the sleight-of-hand involved in the magic was revealed: the fireworks "footprints" were digitally enhanced in the televised images, and the young girl who sang as she soared above the crowd was engaging in aerial karaoke (at the last moment, the girl whose voice was heard on the recording had been deemed too plain to perform by a top Communist Party official). But few in the global audience, estimated at some 2-4 billion, seemed to feel cheated.*

LEFT: MICHAEL MACOR—SAN FRANCISCO CHRONICLE—POLARIS; RIGHT: MARK DADSWELL—GETTY IMAGES

Teammates *At left, swimmers Garrett Weber-Gale, 23, and Michael Phelps, 23, exult after the U.S. team took first place in the 4 x 100-m freestyle relay event. France placed second, and Australia third. The victory earned Phelps the second gold medal of his record-setting eight at the Beijing Games, three of which were won in relay events. Among the benefits of Phelps' aw-shucks personal style was his ability to retain the respect and affection of his teammates, even as his spectacular multimedal feats often overshadowed their strong performances.*

Golden slippers *The Beijing Games produced two superstars, Phelps and Jamaican sprinter Usain Bolt, who, at only 22, swept both the 100- and 200-m sprints in world-record-setting times and helped the Jamaican team win the 4 x 100-m relay, also in record time. An ebullient showman from his gold shoes up, Bolt was so enthused over his triumph in the 100-m race that he began celebrating before he crossed the finish line—yet even so, he set a new world record of 9.69 sec. in the event. Imagine how fast he might run with his shoelaces tied.*

Long and short of it *Above, Americans Misty May-Treanor, 31, left, and Kerri Walsh, 30, celebrate their gold-medal victory over China's Wang Jie and Tian Jia in beach volleyball, a sport that has boomed in popularity since its Olympic debut at the 1996 Atlanta Games.*

Dreamy again *Dwyane Wade, No. 9, runs to join the rest of the U.S. men's basketball team after the Americans beat Spain, 118-107, to win the gold medal. It was a redeeming moment for the U.S. team, following a disappointing third-place finish in the 2004 Athens Games.*

Head over heels *U.S. gymnast Nastia Liukin, 18, soars upside-down in the individual floor exercise event. She placed third but won gold in the most rigorous gymnastics challenge, the all-around event, and also earned three silver medals. She is the daughter of two champion Soviet-era gymnasts who emigrated to the U.S.*

Li Ching

Unsung heroes *Ping-Pong may not seem to be one of sport's more colorful contests—until you try turning the floor red and the tabletop blue. At left, an early table-tennis match in Beijing featured two players from areas very far from favor with China's government: Li Ching of Hong Kong and Chiang Peng-Lung of Taiwan. Other eye-catching events at the Beijing Games included a biracial team from South Africa competing in the canoe/kayak slalom event and an aerial ballet performed by athletes from Japan and France in the women's 63-kg judo event.*

Airborne *At top right, competitors defy gravity in the men's BMX quarterfinals in Beijing. Also catching a breeze are athletes in the windsurfing competition, which was held in the seacoast city of Qingdao, 34 miles southeast of Beijing, where a backdrop of skyscrapers and cranes is testimony to the nation's economic boom.*

At bottom, Lin Dan of China exults after winning the gold medal in badminton, and two Russians demonstrate the discipline that brought them the silver medal in the men's synchronized 3-m springboard diving competition.

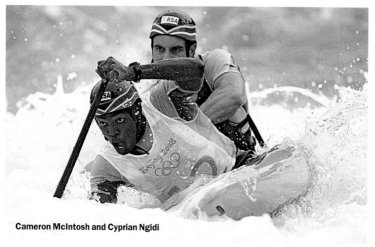

Cameron McIntosh and Cyprian Ngidi

Ayumi Tanimoto and Lucie Decosse

Men's BMX cycling

Men's RS:X-class windsurfing

Lin Dan

Yuriy Kunakov and
Dmitry Sautin

Mariel Zagunis, right (gold); Sada Jacobson, left (silver)

Brian Clay

Phil Dalhausser

U.S. women's soccer team

My summer vacation *Beyond the TV coverage that concentrated on a few popular events— women's beach volleyball, gymnastics and men's swimming—the Beijing Olympics featured a spectacular array of gifted athletes. Here are only a few of the American faces of the Games.*

U.S. women's 400-m relay team: from left, Sanya Richards, Monique Henderson, Allyson Felix, Mary Wineberg

Lisa Leslie

Natalie Coughlin

Harvest of Gold

We can't hail all the victors with a picture, or even a mention, considering all the team winners—but here's a list of most of the U.S. athletes who won individual gold medals at the Beijing Games.

Kristin Armstrong
Women's cycling: individual time trial

Stephanie Brown Trafton
Women's field: discus throw

Bryan Clay
Men's track and field: decathlon

Natalie Coughlin
Women's swimming: 100-m backstroke

Henry Cejudo
Men's wrestling, freestyle: 55-kg class

Phil Dalhausser
Men's beach volleyball

Glenn Eller
Men's shooting: double trap

Vincent Hancock
Men's shooting: skeet

Dawn Harper
Women's track: 100-m hurdles

Shawn Johnson
Women's gymnastics, artistic: balance beam

Ryan Lochte
Men's swimming: 200-m backstroke

LaShawn Merritt
Men's track: 400 m

Aaron Piersol
Men's swimming: 100-m backstroke

Todd Rogers
Men's beach volleyball

Rebecca Soni
Women's swimming: 200-m backstroke

Angelo Taylor
Men's track: 400-m hurdles

Anna Tunnicliffe
Women's sailing, laser radial: one-person dinghy

Mariel Zagunis
Women's fencing: sabre

TEAM GOLD MEDALS
Men's basketball; women's basketball; equestrian team jumping; women's rowing, eight with coxswain; women's soccer; men's volleyball; women's tennis, doubles. Track: men's and women's 4 x 100-m relays; Swimming, men's relays: 4 x 100-m freestyle, 4 x 200-m freestyle, 4 x100-m medley

Science

Big Machine, Tiny Glitch

Behold one section of the new Large
Hadron Collider at the CERN laboratory
in Geneva, which will send beams of
protons hurtling in opposite directions
around a 17-mile underground track at
a minuscule fraction less than the speed
of light—then smash them together.
Physicists will sift through the resulting
atomic debris in hopes of unlocking some
of nature's biggest mysteries, from why
the universe is expanding to how gravity
works. The most sought-after prize: the
Higgs boson, the elusive particle that
many scientists believe gives everything
in the universe its mass.

The collider, beset by delays, took 25
years to plan, $6 billion to build and
involved more than 9,000 scientists from
around the globe. At last, on Sept. 10, it
was fired up for its first test run. But
only nine days later, a tiny electrical
connection between two magnets over-
heated, leading to a minor meltdown
that will likely take the machine offline
until early 2009. Forget the Higgs boson:
Anyone got a fuse?

©CERN

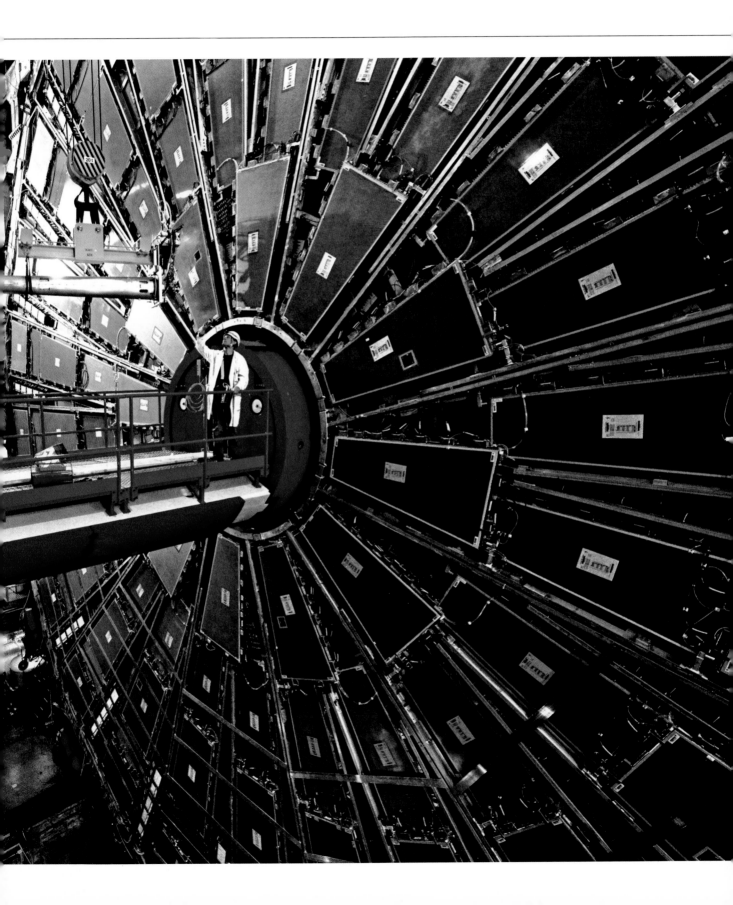

Dr. Nicholas Schiff. He's helping pioneer the use of electrical stimulation to restart damaged brains

I F THERE WERE A SURGICAL PROCEDURE OF THE YEAR, a recent winner would have been an operation known as deep brain stimulation (DBS). Most folks are not familiar with it, but 40,000 people (myself included) are intimately so, having undergone it as a radical—and startlingly effective—way to treat the symptoms of Parkinson's disease. A new frontier in DBS was opened in 2007, when a team led by Dr. Nicholas Schiff of the Weill Cornell Medical College in New York City used it to turn the cognitive lights back on in a man who had spent six years in a near coma as a result of injuries suffered in a mugging and had seemed destined to spend the rest of his life that way.

A DBS procedure is actually two operations. First, surgeons drill a pair of dime-size holes in the skull and thread fine wires down to whatever area of the brain is misfiring or otherwise malfunctioning. A week later, they insert a pacemaker-like device in the chest, thread wires under the skin and connect them to the ones in the brain. When they metaphorically flip the switch (actually, they use magnets to turn the batteries on and off), the

symptoms disappear, or at least are greatly reduced.

For the brain-damaged man in the 2007 procedure, that reduction meant a lot. He is far from cured, but he can recognize his parents and conduct brief conversations. Schiff, 42, led the team that planned and conducted the procedure, though the surgery itself was performed at the Cleveland Clinic by Dr. Ali Rezai, who also performed my procedure and has used DBS on patients with obsessive-compulsive disorder and deep clinical depression. As battlefield medical care gets increasingly sophisticated, more and more soldiers with catastrophic head injuries are surviving combat zones like Iraq, only to come home and find that little can be done to restore their minds. Now, thanks to Schiff and his colleagues, that is changing.

—BY MICHAEL KINSLEY, *TIME* COLUMNIST

'When [doctors] metaphorically flip the switch ... the symptoms disappear or ... are greatly reduced.'

J. Craig Venter. First he built the genetic blueprint for a new life-form. Then he watermarked it

A HALF-CENTURY AFTER THE DISCOVERY OF THE double helix, nobody doubts that it is our DNA that determines what we are—in the same way that lines of code determine software or the digital etchings on a CD determine the music you hear. Etch new signals, and you write a new song. That, in genetic terms, is what J. Craig Venter has done. Working with the four basic nucleotides that make up all DNA, he has assembled an entirely new chromosome for an entirely new one-celled creature. Insert that genome into a cell—like inserting a disc into a computer—and a new species of living thing will be booted up. Venter hasn't done that yet. What he appears to have done, however, is crack the manufacturing code. Once that's done, there may be little limit to what you can eventually build.

A restless, underachieving student in California, Venter served in Vietnam as a Navy hospital corpsman and returned to the U.S. determined to practice medicine. Instead, in medical school he became enthralled by biochemistry and ended up taking a job with the National Institutes of Health (NIH) in Washington. Ambitious and freethinking, he detested the bureaucratic maze and longed for the opportunity to test his innovative ideas for transforming the emerging field of genetics. In 1992 he created his own company, the Institute for Genomic Research. Within three years he completed the first genome sequencing of an entire organism, the bacterium that causes meningitis.

Venter's firm became a go-to place for sequencing projects, and soon he was hungering for the biggest prize in biology: the map of the human genome. It was a project of mind-numbing complexity, but Venter brainstormed a way to automate the process, and in 2000, after a feverish competition, he finished mapping the genome just ahead of the government's $3 billion sequencing effort, led by Dr. Francis Collins.

During a two-year hiatus from his firm, Venter began wondering, What is the minimum genome an organism needs to survive and reproduce? And could he build it? Not only did his team succeed in building their own bacterium, they also took the opportunity to rewrite its genetic score. First, they introduced a mutation that would prevent it from causing disease. Then they branded it with watermarks to distinguish it as a product of their lab, using a code built around selected genes to embed their names within it. The next step will be to insert the gene into a cell and see if it indeed stirs to life. —BY ALICE PARK

'Soon he was hungering for the biggest prize in biology: the map of the human genome.'

Paydirt *In September, as the summer season ended in the northern hemisphere of Mars, NASA scientists prepared to test soil from the "Snow White" trench at left, dug by the Phoenix lander's robotic arm. The probe held four onboard chemical tests, which added purified water from Earth to Martian soil and then baked and analyzed it.*

Cosmic Flock

The solar system is filled with NASA's plucky probes: in 2008 they had a very good year

FOR ALL THE ATTENTION THAT THE SHUTTLE, THE space station and other manned spacecraft get, the real foot soldiers of space exploration have always been the unmanned ships—and right now they're enjoying something of a golden age. The U.S. currently has no fewer than 11 interplanetary probes scattered about the solar system; five are orbiting, roving or approaching Mars alone, and the others are targeting Mercury, the sun, Saturn and numerous comets or asteroids.

Three of the rugged ships stood out from the rest in 2008: the Cassini Saturn orbiter, the Ulysses solar surveyor and the Phoenix Mars lander. Cassini was the first to take center stage. On March 12, near Saturn, the orbiter executed a dramatic dive through an icy geyser that reaches 950 miles (1,530 km) into space from the

Saturnian moon Enceladus. Passing just 120 miles (190 km) above the lunar surface, Cassini sampled the icy exhaust that researchers didn't even know existed until the spacecraft spotted it in 2005. Seven more close-brush flybys of the moon are in the offing, including one high-wire plunge that will drop the spacecraft a scant 15 miles (24 km) above Enceladus' surface. Later in the year, Cassini, launched by NASA's Jet Propulsion Laboratory, made an unusually high orbit above Saturn's massive B ring, capturing unique new images of the ring, spread like an immense halo around the planet.

NASA and the European Space Agency planned to retire their Ulysses solar surveyor on March 30, as its nuclear-powered generator was running out of fuel. But the orbiter seemed reluctant to take its last bow: it kept limp-

FROM TOP: NASA—JOHNS HOPKINS UNIVERSITY APPLIED PHYSICS LABORATORY—CARNEGIE INSTITUTION OF WASHINGTON; JPL—NASA VIA AP IMAGES; JPL—CALTECH—U. OF ARIZONA—NASA; EUROPEAN SPACE AGENCY —ESOC

ing along, and NASA kept extending the estimates of its final shutdown.

If it swirls, floats or emanates near our closest star, Ulysses studied it. Among other achievements, the surveyor took the first full measure of the sun's polar regions. The spacecraft also discovered that the sun's magnetic field determines the regions that produce the solar wind, and ruffled more than a few scientists' feathers when it showed that a hot corona produces the fastest solar winds—exactly the opposite of prevailing theories. Ulysses also tracked interstellar dust particles all the way from the sun to Earth and in so doing helped map the planet's magnetic fields.

The year's high point arrived on May 25, when NASA's Phoenix lander touched down in Mars' arctic region. The lander hoped to offer a first look at actual Martian water ice, rather than the dry water scars of millenniums past. Using a digging arm and a suite of mineralogy instruments, the lander hunted for salts, clays and other signs that liquid water is manipulating the soil. On July 31, scientists confirmed that the lander's robotic arm had dug up a soil sample that revealed the presence of subsurface water ice. The lander's onboard geology lab also identified the Martian soil in the region as slightly alkaline.

NASA has ambitious plans for further unmanned missions. The Lunar Reconnaissance Orbiter (LRO), scheduled to launch in April 2009, will conduct the most comprehensive surveys of the moon the U.S. has ever attempted, using cameras that can spot an object as small as a football. The mission will help scout for landing sites, as NASA is holding fast to its plans to return astronauts to the moon by 2020. It will also collect detailed images of all six Apollo landing sites, unseen for close to 40 years. "Right now we have a view from the 1970s, and here we are in the 21st century," said Jim Garvin, chief scientist at NASA's Goddard's Space Flight Center, where the craft is being assembled.

More missions to Mars are anticipated, including one that would return soil samples and allow NASA to rehearse the round-trip skills that would be necessary for a manned mission. And even as the new ships are readied, some of the great historic ones are still in flight. Voyagers 1 and 2, launched in 1977 on a grand tour of the outer planets, are now on their way out of the solar system, with the last breaths of solar wind at their backs. Remarkably, NASA may be able to stay in touch with them for up to 30 more years—meaning the granddaddy probes could remain online long after some of the newest ones have winked out. —BY DAN CRAY

What's Flying Now

NASA's ships are everywhere, from the sun to Saturn and en route to Pluto. The celestial fleet includes four superstar probes

MESSENGER

Launched toward Mercury in 2004, the probe will enter orbit in 2011 but made two flybys of the planet in 2008. In the fall, it sent high-quality pictures of the side of Mercury never seen before, including this Oct. 6 image. It also discovered water in Mercury's exosphere—to the astonishment of planetary scientists—and indicated heavy volcanic activity in the planet's past.

ULYSSES

The NASA-European Space Agency probe was losing power and slated to be retired at the end of March 2008, as its nuclear generator ran out of fuel. But the orbiter just kept on ticking and was still powered up, if feebly, as of Nov. 1, 2008.

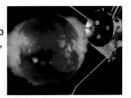

PHOENIX

Joining four other U.S. probes currently orbiting or roving Mars, the lander touched down near the Martian north pole (illustrated above) and began deploying its robotic arm to dig up soil samples, which it then tested in its internal chemistry lab. Along with discovering minerals suggesting the planet's surface once held liquid seas, Phoenix also detected snowfall on Mars.

CASSINI

Orbiting Saturn since 2004, it has studied the planet's rings and landed a probe on one of its moons. In 2008 it flew through an icy geyser on the Saturnine moon Enceladus—a feature unknown until Cassini discovered it in a 2005 flyby.

Nature's Savagery

Earthquakes, floods, cyclones and hurricanes: scenes from the year's worst natural disasters

Scavenger *Above, a young man carries a mattress amid the ruins of Yingxiu, in China's southwest province of Sichuan, several weeks after a 7.9-magnitude earthquake struck the densely populated region on May 12, killing an estimated 70,000 and leaving as many as 5 million people homeless. The government reacted quickly to the most powerful quake to strike China since 1976, sending some 100,000 relief workers to the province.*

Trapped *At right, rescuers work to free a student from the ruins of Wudu Primary School in Mianzhu City. The quake exposed the substandard construction of many structures built during China's recent boom years.*

Flotsam *A monster cyclone ravaged Burma (or Myanmar, as the clique of repressive generals that rules the nation prefers to call it), on May 2-3, killing more than 130,000 people and leaving millions of Burmese in dire need of food, potable water and medical aid. Yet even as a U.S. Navy ship loaded with supplies hovered offshore and rescue workers from global relief agencies stood by to assist, the regime impeded their efforts to help—and did not even send the nation's military to the aid of its desperate citizens. At left, young men in Rangoon troll for flotsam after the storm.*

Stranded *Below, refugees from monsoon floods seek refuge in southern India in May. When the rains reached northern India, they caused the region's worst flooding in 50 years. The final toll: 1,000 dead and 5 million left homeless.*

Storm warnings *In late August, Americans braced for a replay of the horrors of Hurricane Katrina as Hurricane Gustav made a beeline for New Orleans. Mayor Ray Nagin ordered the city evacuated, and the Bush Administration, still reeling from its inept response to Katrina, went on high alert. Fortunately, the storm weakened and the city escaped major damage. At right, floodwaters splash over the banks of the Crescent City's Industrial Canal on Sept. 1.*

Only days later, a stronger storm, Hurricane Ike, struck the Texas coast after ravaging Haiti and other islands in the Caribbean. The Category 2 storm wreaked its worst havoc on Galveston and Houston. Above, beach houses burn on hard-hit Galveston Island. Ike's U.S. toll: 70 dead and $12 billion in damages.

Floods *Following spring rains that were far heavier than usual, swollen rivers in Iowa strained the state's levees, bursting dozens of them. Iowa's second largest city, Cedar Rapids (pop. 124,000), and one of its smallest towns, Chelsea (pop. 276), were inundated. At right, volunteers in Oakville (pop. 439) stuff sandbags on the night of June 16 to save the town's dike. The structure failed, and the town was flooded, leaving some of the locals, above, without homes.*

The massive tide swept through Illinois, Missouri, Indiana and points downstream but spared St. Louis, where it peaked at 9 ft. below the floodwall. The toll: more than 24 dead and damages estimated at $8 billion.

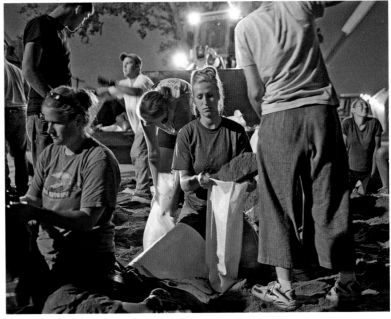

Briefing

No-span zone *Residents of New Hampshire still mourn the loss of the Granite State's signature rock feature, the Old Man of the Mountain, obliterated by a 2003 rockslide. Across the continent, another landmark was lost in 2008: on Aug. 4, Wall Arch, one of the most famous landmarks in Arches National Park in Utah, succumbed to the gravity it had long defied.*

Saving the Planet? It's in the Bag

In a greening world, reusable shopping bags are becoming as essential as a shopping list. According to market-research company NPD's Accessories Tracker, sales for reusable shopping totes rose 72% in the period between January 2007 through May 2008. In 2007, Eco-Bags Products in Ossining, N.Y., generated sales of $2.2 million, a 300% increase over the prior year.

Grocery giant Whole Foods Market stopped using plastic bags in April 2008, and has "sold in excess of 2 million reusable bags in many styles," said Michael Besancon, who heads the retailer's green initiative. Mona Williams, who oversees the buying department at the Container Store, told TIME that after the company introduced a recycled, reusable tote, "sales have been amazing. Consumer attitudes toward reusables have radically changed. It's not a fad. It's a lifestyle change."

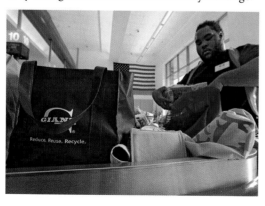

Booting Big Sugar from the Everglades

Can the Everglades come back from the dead? At a June 24 news conference near the imperiled "River of Grass," Florida Governor Charlie Crist announced a $1.75 billion deal to buy the U.S. Sugar Corp., including 187,000 acres (75,677 hectares) of farmland that once comprised the northern Everglades. The deal was designed to extinguish a powerful 77-year-old company (with 1,700 employees) and deep roots in South Florida's coal-black organic soil, in hopes of resurrecting and reconfiguring a moribund eight-year-old Everglades replumbing effort that is supposed to be the most ambitious ecosystem-restoration project in the history of the planet.

The purchase would give the state control of nearly half the 400,000 acres (161,876 hectares) of sugar fields in the Everglades Agricultural Area (EAA) below Lake Okeechobee. But as details of the plan emerged, officials said only about half the land the state would acquire from the company would be ecologically restored; the rest likely will remain in agriculture. A congressionally mandated report issued in late September again underscored that the vast wetland is in dire peril and called for immediate action to stop further degradation.

Hold the Veggies—but Which Ones?

A salmonella outbreak that began in April infected more than 1,400 people and hospitalized more than 285 in 43 states. Relying on reports from those afflicted, the Food and Drug Administration (FDA) warned that some tomatoes were unsafe, and grocers were forced to dump tons of unsold, spoiling produce. Yet that didn't stop the bug, and it was not until late July that the FDA fingered the real culprit: Mexican-grown jalapeño and seranno peppers. Outraged tomato growers said hasty action by the federal agency cost them millions in lost revenues.

Seeds for the Future

It's a maxim as true for farming as it is for your home PC: always back up your data. In agriculture, data take the form of seeds, and to ensure that a doomsday for blossoms never comes, an international seed bank built into a mountain on a Norwegian island in the Arctic opened in February. The Svalbard Global Seed Vault will eventually be expanded to include genetic samples of every crop on the planet. The structure below is the entrance to the bank, most of which extends under the surface of the ice-covered island, where specimens will be kept dry at around 0°F.

Warming to The Kindle

For years we've been told that the future of reading is digital. But it took the full heft of online marketing giant Amazon and its boss, Jeff Bezos, below, to make the first portable reading device that is becoming a hit with consumers, the Kindle.

TIME technology writer Josh Quittner, a self-confessed gadget geek, admitted that he hated the Kindle when he first tested it, but "like Beauty,

I found myself carried away by the quiet virtues of the Beast: how the Kindle feels encased in creamy leather, the way the gadget helps me power through a book superfast and how it lets me take my library on a plane. Best of all is books on demand—delivered in seconds to the kitchen table on Sunday as I read the weekly book reviews."

Since You Asked . . .

Neil deGrasse Tyson.

The director of New York City's Hayden Planetarium replies to our readers' queries

What should be done about the fact that American children lag behind kids in other countries in science and math?

Francis Harrington, MARLBOROUGH, MASS.

We need to do something about the stigma. Somehow it's O.K. for people to chuckle about not being good at math. Yet if I said I never learned to read, they'd say I was an illiterate dolt. Science and math [are] fundamental to what it is to be alive, because they're all around us.

If you could meet any scientist who ever lived, who would it be?

Larry Bassett, THORNWOOD, N.Y.

Isaac Newton. No question about it. The smartest person ever to walk the face of this earth. The man was connected to the universe in spooky ways. He discovered the laws of motion, the laws of gravity, the laws of optics. Then he turned 26.

Is man fully capable of under-standing the universe's design?

Bruan Lendl Ong, MANILA

I lose sleep at night wondering whether we are intelligent enough to figure out the universe. I don't know.

Arts

SEATTLE ART MUSEUM, GIFT OF ROBERT M. ARNOLD, IN HONOR OF THE 75TH ANNIVERSARY OF THE SEATTLE ART MUSEUM, 2006. EXHIBITION COPY INSTALLED AT SOLOMON R. GUGGENHEIM MUSEUM, NEW YORK, 2008 © SOLOMON R. GUGGENHEIM FOUNDATION NEW YORK. PHOTO BY DAVID HEALD

M.P.G.: 24 Highway, 36 Museum

Born in Mao Zedong's China, artist Cai Guo-Qiang, 50, knows all about societies in transformation, a subject he addresses in such theatrical installations as *Head On*, in which dozens of papier-mâché wolves gallop headlong into a glass wall. He has also produced outdoor "explosion events," using fireworks to create elaborate, fleeting aerial spectacles.

In 2008 the Solomon R. Guggenheim Museum in New York City staged a clamorous mid-career retrospective, "Cai Guo-Qiang: I Want to Believe." TIME art critic Richard Lacayo hailed the show's "big bang" feel but found fault with its central work, *Innopportune: Stage One*—a car-bombing presented as a Chinese-scroll sequence of tumbling automobiles, blinking light rods bursting from them like fireworks—suspended down the length of the building's vast rotunda. "It's an instance of an artist playing air guitar with history," Lacayo wrote, "making a strenuous gesture to create the impression that he's summoning a powerful reality, when in fact he's merely toyed with it."

Robert Downey Jr. Iron Man? More like Actor Man, who discovered greatness by choosing bravely

GOT TO DIRECT ROBERT DOWNEY JR. IN *TROPIC THUNDER*, and he took on a role that few would have had the courage to tackle and, I am now convinced, none could have played except him. Yes, Downey, 43, is Iron Man, but he really is Actor Man. And also, by the way, a genius. In the realm where box office is irrelevant and talent is king, the realm that actually means something, he has always ruled, and finally in the summer of 2008 he got to have his cake and let us eat him up all the way to the multiplex, where his mastery was in full effect in both *Iron Man* and *Thunder*.

Now, the genius thing can be off-putting because ... how do you act with a genius? How do you direct a genius? Maybe, I secretly hoped, he really isn't such a genius and I will find out that—hah!—it is all just a lot of hype, it's all charisma and editing. Wrong. First day at work—definitely a genius, playing a Method actor from Australia playing an African-American soldier in an over-the-top Vietnam War movie within a movie and never breaking character (in the movie). He riffs, he

improvises, he is funnier than the script most of the time.

What it takes to be an actor, good or bad, is a bravery of sorts. Downey's choices are as brave as they come. He is not afraid to try something fully, knowing it could end in disaster but also understanding that that is where greatness lies. Many actors do this, but so few with the underlying sensitivity and facility with their emotions that he has.

I was an admirer of his before I worked with him. Now I feel, as if by some gift from a higher power, Robert Downey Jr. was sent down to Earth to help us all realize (through his work) that the human experience is a sad, funny, beautiful thing, full of imperfection and irony. I have had a chance to work with one of the greats, and he tricked me into actually thinking I was keeping up.

—BY BEN STILLER, *director*, Tropic Thunder

Maybe, I secretly hoped, he really isn't such a genius ... Wrong. First day at work—definitely a genius

Ricky Gervais. Ever wonder who the artist of pumped-up pomposity employs for a model?

BEFORE WE WALK INTO THE GALLERIES OF THE GETTY Museum, Ricky Gervais feels the need to lean against a railing overlooking the hills of Los Angeles and quote Keats' *When I Have Fears That I May Cease to Be*. At length. "I know what he means now," he says. "You hit an age and you realize, What is your legacy? And you don't want to waste your time on things that you're not proud of." Dude, I'm thinking, let's go make fun of paintings! But I can't stop him.

Luckily, it lasts only 10 minutes, and then we're inside, and Gervais proves to be the best person in the world to go to a museum with. He has a shocking knowledge of art history, gets swoony over tiny details and moves very quickly. And yes, he makes fun of paintings. Could it be that Gervais takes the piss out of arrogance because there's so much of it in him? That self-assurance is why he's been turning down movie roles ever since the second episode of *The Office*, the hit British sitcom that launched his career. He had no interest in starring in a film he didn't have complete creative control over. His 2008 movie, *Ghost Town*—a small, hilarious romantic comedy about a dyspeptic dentist— marked the first time Gervais took a major role in a movie he didn't write and direct. He's working on a movie with his writing partner on *The Office* and *Extras*, Stephen Merchant, about a group of twentysomething friends in 1970s England trying to escape from their poor, small town. That's what Gervais did, leaving Reading, England, to go to college and then play in a rock band, eventually getting a job in radio when he was 36.

Now Gervais and his girlfriend, whom he met in college, live in London and have a second home on Manhattan's Upper East Side, because it's close to the museums. At 47, he still has the impishness of someone who unexpectedly made it. When he spots a sign pointing upstairs to paintings, the L.A.-ness of it cracks him up. "'Paintings!' That's great. They have to be very specific. Like 'Things Made of Clay.'"—BY JOEL STEIN

At 47, he still has the impishness of someone who unexpectedly made it

Curtain Up! Broadway welcomes a new wunderkind and restores the luster to a pair of musical classics

Tops: *In the Heights* Lin-Manuel Miranda, only 28, is the conceiver, composer, lyricist and star of this warm, upbeat slice of street life set in a Dominican Manhattan neighborhood. Result: both hip and wholesome.

Divine diva: *Gypsy* Patti LuPone, Broadway's original Evita and a zesty Reno Sweeny in Anything Goes, *enjoyed a titanic star turn and snagged a Tony Award in a fine production of (another!) revival of* Gypsy.

Revitalized: *South Pacific* Finally back on Broadway, the 1949 Rodgers and Hammerstein classic looked surprisingly fresh, astringent, meaty and convention-defying. As for the music and lyrics: wondrous.

Rock, rap, remember. R.E.M. roars back, Coldplay stays hot and in rap's domain it's the reign of Wayne

Comeback: R.E.M. *For years its music was short on purpose and energy, but R.E.M. rekindled its drive with the CD* Accelerate, *trading its long musical bridges to nowhere for new, high-energy riffs.*

On top: Lil Wayne *New Orleans native Dwayne Carter Jr. fuses thrilling wordplay with a unique delivery. With* Tha Carter III, *the prolific poet proved his boast: he's the best rapper alive.*

Rising: Coldplay *The British lads have sold 31 million albums, won four Grammys and, with U2 and Radiohead, are part of adult-rock's holy trinity. And Coldplay's new CD,* Viva la Vida, *was a hit. But go figure: it's still uncool to admit you like Chris Martin & Co.*

Dark Knight, Bright Box Office *Director Christopher Nolan, Christian Bale, above, as Bruce Wayne and an inspired Heath Ledger as the Joker teamed up to make* The Dark Knight, *Nolan's second chapter in his revival of the DC Comics Batman franchise, into Hollywood's fourth biggest hit in history (worldwide gross as of October 2008: $988 million). Said* TIME *critic Richard Corliss: "It's been one of the best summers in memory for flat-out blockbuster entertainment, and in the wow category, the Nolan film doesn't disappoint. But Nolan has a more subversive agenda. He wants viewers to stick their hands down the rat hole of evil and see if they get bitten.* The Dark Knight *is beyond dark: it's as black—and teeming and toxic—as the mind of the Joker."*

Of Sexes and Multiplexes. Big-screen gender-blender: ladies singing Abba battle gentlemen in weird costumes

Chick Flicks Move Tix *They're on the move: not only the stars who brought the Broadway and TV hits* Mamma Mia! *and* Sex and the City *to the multiplex but also the millions of women who lined up to see them, especially the Cosmo-hoisting fans of the latter, based on the long-running* HBO *series. Of Sarah Jessica Parker and her three sassy friends,* TIME's *Corliss noted: "In* SATC, *as in fashion magazines like* Vogue *and* IN STYLE, *the editorial is indistinguishable from the advertising. You can't tell where the drama ends and the product placement begins." And though Meryl Streep led the* MM *cast, Corliss found its real star was the music of Abba, the '70s Swedish quartet that "created the ... most buoyant body of work from any pop group since the Beatles." His verdict: "Great music—weird movie."*

Indy Fatigable *They're back! Steven Spielberg, George Lucas, Harrison Ford and newcomer Shia LaBeouf, above right, teamed up to make the fourth in a classic series. Corliss found some parts creaky but wrote:* "Indiana Jones and the Kingdom of the Crystal Skull ... *works effectively, as instant nostalgia—a class reunion of the old gang who in the '80s reinvigorated the classic action film with such expertise and brio ... Ford looks just fine and seems sprightlier than the rest of the movie."*

Feel the Burn *Corliss:* "Burn After Reading *finds Ethan and Joel Cohen back on familiar, strange terrain, where people talk smart and act stupid and a moviegoer doesn't know whether to laugh or ... not laugh. Brad Pitt, as an oafish gym rat, has the sharpest, sweetest role of his career ... The film will keep you guessing: not just what happens next, but what game the Coens are playing."*

Irony Man *"POW! BANG! KA-BOOM! It's* Iron Man *to the rescue," wrote Corliss of the latest Hollywood franchise derived from Marvel Comics, "yanking movies and the worldwide box office out of its months-long doldrums and into the stratosphere ... The real treat is for grownups, who get a beguiling character study behind and above the special effects." (In the title role), "Robert Downey Jr. is Irony Man, standing off to the side, undercutting the hero's big dreams or rash motives with a sardonic critique delivered at lightning speed."*

Briefing

ESSENTIAL STORIES

Poperator *For more than a decade, Briton Damien Hirst has been one of the richest and most famous artists in the world. But in 2008 he outdid himself—and shook up the art market—by staging a two-day sale of 223 works at Sotheby's in London, the first time any auction house has sold a quantity of work fresh from an artist's studio. Total receipts of the sale, which included such Hirst works as* The Golden Calf, *a white bullock preserved in a tank of formaldehyde with horns and hooves of 18-karat gold, and* The Incredible Journey, *above, a preserved zebra: $200 million. Ka-ching!*

Clean Sweep

For only the second time in the history of the Academy Awards, foreign stars swept the four Oscar awards for acting. Savoring their big night, below, are Daniel Day-Lewis (Best Actor, *There Will Be Blood*), Tilda Swinton (Best Supporting Actress, *Michael Clayton),* Marion Cotillard (Best Actress, *La Vie en Rose)* and Javier Bardem (Best Supporting Actor, *No Country for Old Men). Bravissimo!*

Minimalist modernism *"Broad, flat, pale and gray may not sound like a formula for pleasure. But you don't know what pleasure is until you've seen Japanese architect Tadao Ando's Church of the Light near Osaka, Japan," wrote* TIME *architecture critic Richard Lacayo. On June 22 Ando's Stone Hill Center, above, a combination of galleries and art-conservation labs, opened in Williamstown, Mass. Lacayo's verdict: "It's pale, gray, serene, economical, subdued and, from most angles, pretty splendid."*

Pacific overtures *Call it Gershwin diplomacy: late in February the New York Philharmonic visited North Korea and played a concert, in a breakthrough for U.S. relations with Kim Jong Il's isolated, impoverished nation.* TIME's *Bill Powell, one of 80 journalists who accompanied the orchestra, found the concert deeply moving, but noted, "The North Koreans, to say the least, are control freaks." Even so, wrote Powell, signs of the nation's repression and poverty were everywhere.*

A Mad, Mad Ad World

In its first season, AMC's *Mad Men*, a drama set in an ad agency in the 1960s, won two Golden Globes and six Emmy awards, becoming the first basic-cable series to win an Emmy for Outstanding Drama Series. Said TIME's James Poniewozik: "*Mad Men*... is deliciously curated ... but the subtle, deliberately paced drama has a wider sense of history. [Main character Don Draper, played by Jon Hamm, seated] is an American archetype of self-reinvention, a Gatsby or a Huck Finn, who lights out for the territory but cannot escape from himself."

Move Over, Harry P.

Like one of the vampires she writes about, Stephenie Meyer has turned into something rare and more than merely human: a literary phenomenon. The Phoenix housewife, 34, had never written much before a vivid 2003 dream about a vampire inspired her to write a young adult novel called *Twilight*, which she followed up with two sequels.

Together the three books have sold more than 5 million copies. Meyer's latest vampire novel, *Breaking Dawn*, was published in August and sold more than 1 million copies in its first day on sale.

"Smart, funny and cheery," noted TIME book critic Lev Grossman, "Meyer does not seem noticeably undead in person." The observant Mormon, a teetotaler, takes pains to eschew drinking, smoking and sex in her novels, but, as Grossman observed, "... they're about the erotics of abstinence. Their tension comes from prolonged, superhuman acts of self-restraint."

Since You Asked ...

Helen Mirren. The regal actress replies to readers' queries

What was the most difficult point in your career?

Matthias Kruzik, VIENNA, AUSTRIA

I think probably my mid-30s, which was the one time really when it should have been the best because I was experienced and ready, and the kind of work that I wanted to do just didn't come my way. But you, know, you just carry on ... regardless. I would just do whatever work came my way.

Do you think it's important for celebrities to contribute their two cents on political, ethical and economic problems?

Amanda Cusick, PIEDMONT, CALIF.

I've used my voice to publicize certain issues. I've been involved with Oxfam on the proliferation of the illegal sale of small arms throughout the world, which is causing such, such devastation, and the war in northern Uganda. The only way you can sometimes garner attention is by sending someone like me as a front person.

You have a tattoo on your hand. What is it, and why did you get it?

Charles Adkins, AVENTURA, FLA.

The short answer is, I got drunk. It's a South American Indian sign.

Milestones

APPRECIATION

Tim Russert, 1950-2008

BACK WHEN HE WAS JUST STARTING IN TELEVISION—
and ever since, but particularly back then—Tim
Russert was astounded by the joys of the job. Early on,
he helped arrange an interview with the Pope for the
Today show—and Tim did it up right: he took along
red NBC News baseball caps for the Cardinals and a
white one for the Holy Father. "He put it on!" Tim told
me when he came home. "We have pictures." Then he
said, more quietly, "But you know, it was really something being in his presence. You felt something holy. It
was almost as if the air was different." And that was
Tim—exuberant, irreverent, brilliant and devout, a

thrilling jolt of humanity. We were friends for 30 years.

Tim was proudly, indelibly Irish—not only in his
early beer-drinking years but also in his more Jesuiti-
cal incarnation as the host of *Meet the Press*, when he
refused to socialize on Saturday nights. And yet, even
at the top of his profession, he never lost track of his
roots—in part because he never lost track of his dad,
Big Russ, a Buffalo, N.Y., sanitation worker who was
the subject of his admiring 2004 memoir *Big Russ and
Me*, who survives him. Tim would review his Sunday
questions with Big Russ in mind, always asking himself, What would Dad want to know? —BY JOE KLEIN

'That was Tim Russert—exuberant,
irreverent, brilliant and devout—
a thrilling jolt of humanity.'
—JOE KLEIN, TIME POLITICAL COLUMNIST

Cyd Charisse, 1922-2008

IN THE GOLDEN AGE OF THE HOLLYWOOD MUSI-
cal, actress and dancer Charisse shimmered.
The Texas native, who changed her name from
Tula Ellice Finklea, had a series of small roles
until she wowed audiences with her lithe yet
sultry performance alongside Gene Kelly in
1952's *Singin' in the Rain.* Known for her never-
ending legs, Charisse soon became a sought-
after partner, often paired with Kelly or Fred
Astaire. She captivated audiences in a string of
hit movie musicals, including *Brigadoon* (1954)
and *The Band Wagon* (1953), below, in which
she had her first starring role.

Bo Diddley, 1928-2008

APPORTIONING CREDIT FOR THE INVENTION OF ROCK 'N' ROLL
among Chuck Berry, Little Richard, Jerry Lee Lewis and a few
other pioneers has always been a challenge. Suffice it to say
that Bo Diddley never thought he got enough—and he was
right. Born Otha Ellas Bates in Mississippi, Diddley moved to
Chicago as a child and learned to make violins and guitars in
vocational school before dropping out to play music. He took
the stage name Bo Diddley, slang for a bowlegged fool, and his
first recording for Chess Records, *Bo Diddley* (1955), rocketed
to No.1 on the Billboard R&B chart and introduced the world
to rock's defining rhythm, the "hambone" beat that's fueled
everything from Buddy Holly's *Not Fade Away* to U2's *Desire*
to the White Stripes' *Screwdriver.*   —BY JOSH TYRANGIEL

Robert Mondavi, 1913-2008

HE ENDURED A BITTER SPLIT WITH HIS FAMILY, THE EARLY
snubs of oenophiles and ultimately a corporate buyout, but
along the way the pioneering California vintner showed the
world that good wine isn't just the province of Provence. In
1966, after being expelled from the family business, Robert
Mondavi founded his own winery. At the time, American
wine was considered the dregs of the global industry.
Mondavi changed that, turning his winery into one of the
nation's largest and transforming California's Napa Valley
into one of the world's premier winemaking regions.

APPRECIATION

Paul Newman, 1925-2008

I FIRST MET PAUL NEWMAN IN 1968, WHEN GEORGE ROY Hill, the director of *Butch Cassidy and the Sundance Kid*, introduced us in New York City. When the studio didn't want me for the film—it wanted somebody as well known as Paul—he stood up for me. I don't know how many people would have done that; they would have listened to their agents or the studio powers.

The friendship that grew out of the experience of making that film and *The Sting* four years later had its genesis in the fact that although there was an age difference, we both came from a tradition of theater and live TV. We were respectful of craft and focused on digging into the characters we were going to play. Both of us were fundamentally American actors, with the qualities and virtues that characterize American actors: irreverence, playing on the other's flaws for fun, one-upmanship—but always with an underlying affection. Those were also at the core of our relationship off the screen.

Paul was very engaged at work. He was there. He liked a lot of rehearsal. But he was fun too. When he'd make a

mistake, he would enjoy it more than anybody. I'd look at him, and he'd look at me, and I'd say, "You're not fooling anybody. You're not staring at me intensely; you've lost your line." And he'd roar with laughter.

We shared the belief that if you're fortunate enough to have success, you should put something back—he with his Newman's Own food and his Hole in the Wall camps for kids who are gravely ill, and me with Sundance and the institute and the festival. Paul and I didn't see each other all that regularly, but sharing that brought us together. We supported each other financially and by showing up at events. And then we'd give each other a hard time. If you're in a position of being viewed iconically, you'd better have a mechanism to take yourself down to keep the balance. I think we did that for each other.

What impressed me about Paul was that he was very realistic about who he was. He knew the world of hyperbole and distortion he was in. That meant he maintained a certain amount of privacy. He was generous and a pillar of integrity. He was loyal and self-effacing. His commitment to his profession was serious, as was his commitment to social responsibility and especially to his family. He had a life that had real meaning and that will for some time.

I last saw him a few months before his death. He'd been in and out of the hospital. I knew what the deal was, and he knew what the deal was, and we didn't talk about it. Ours was a relationship that didn't need a lot of words.

Mostly I'll miss the fun we had. We played lots of pranks on each other. I used to race cars, and after he took this rare Porsche I owned for a drive, he began to get into racing. He had incredible reflexes, and he got really good, but he talked so much about it that I got sick of it. So I had a beaten-up Porsche shell delivered to his porch for his 50th birthday. He never said anything, but not long after, I found a crate of molten metal delivered to the living room of my (rented) house. It dented the floor. I then had it turned into a really ugly sculpture and dropped into his garden. To his last day, neither one of us ever mentioned it. —BY ROBERT REDFORD

Aleksandr Solzhenitsyn, 1918-2008

ONE DAY IN THE LIFE OF IVAN DENISOVICH, ALEKSANDR Solzhenitsyn's searing account of the Soviet-labor camp experience, found favor during Nikita Khrushchev's short-lived thaw and was published in 1962. By the time the temperature chilled again, Solzhenitsyn's international fame was such that he could not be altogether dispensed with. In 1974, when the Brezhnev regime decided it would not tolerate the foreign publication of *The Gulag Archipelago*, the writer's expansive yet detailed history of the labor camps, Solzhenitsyn was arrested and put on a plane. He breathed a little easier when the plane took off westward and not toward Siberia.

Exiled in Vermont, where he lived from 1976 until his return to a post-Soviet Russia in 1994, Solzhenitsyn was disciplined and unwavering: bearing witness to millions of terrorized voices does not allow for writer's block, nor does it allow for vacations. —BY RADHIKA JONES

William F. Buckley Jr., 1925-2008

IF BEING A CONSERVATIVE ALWAYS LED TO A LIFE LIKE WILLIAM F. BUCKLEY Jr.'s, there would be no more liberals left. Who imagined that the life of the mind could be so damn fun? The mansions and yachts, the cocktails and cigars, the fabulous wife, the *Who's Who* of friends, the bottomless supply of anecdotes and witty ripostes—and, somehow wedged in, enough career accomplishments for five large lives.

Buckley played a key role in the signal political phenomenon of late 20th century America: the rise of conservatism. The wealthy young man nominated himself chief spokesman for the conservative movement, then leveraged his investment with energy, passion and cheerful relentlessness. He wrote books laying out the conservative worldview; launched a magazine, *National Review*, to nurture and promote its values; and created the PBS show *Firing Line*, laying the groundwork for countless pundits who followed. —BY DAVID VON DREHLE

Maharishi Mahesh Yogi
1917-2008

THE BEATLES SEALED THEIR GURU'S fame when they visited his Indian ashram in 1968, but in the end, Transcendental Meditation founder Maharishi Mahesh Yogi may have regretted the association. The gray-haired guru nurtured TM—the practice of exploring consciousness through meditation and chanting—into a multimillion-dollar global business. But he was said to have become uncomfortable with its drug-using counter-culture fan base. John Lennon, in turn, parodied the guru in a scathing screed on the White Album, *Sexy Sadie.*

Sir Edmund Hillary, 1920-2008

FOR ONE WHO HAD REACHED SUCH A LOFTY HEIGHT, HE WAS A strange mix of confidence and modesty. A beekeeper from New Zealand, Edmund Hillary was an aggressive amateur mountaineer drawn, he said, by the appeal of "grinding [competitors] into the ground on a big hill." Yet after accomplishing one of the 20th century's defining feats—his conquest, with Nepalese Sherpa Tenzing Norgay *(above right)*, of Mount Everest on May 29, 1953— he channeled the attention and knighthood that followed toward aiding the Nepalese Sherpas, who had so often helped him. Raising funds through his Himalayan Trust, Hillary helped install pipes and bridges and built 30 schools, two hospitals, 12 medical clinics and more. The arduous work didn't faze him. In 1996 he told TIME, "I would like to see myself not going [to Nepal] quite so often. But at the moment ... the responsibility is there. It has to be done." —BY SIMON ROBINSON

Roy Scheider, 1932-2008

HE HAD ONE OF THE MOST FAMOUS LINES in movie history. As embattled police chief Martin Brody in Steven Spielberg's 1975 blockbuster *Jaws*, Roy Scheider at last sees the 25-ft. great white and says to shark hunter Quint: "You're gonna need a bigger boat." The ex-boxer first got attention, and an Oscar nomination, as Gene Hackman's partner in *The French Connection* (1971) and proved he could be vulnerable as choreographer Joe Gideon in Bob Fosse's semiautobiographical *All That Jazz* (1979), a role for which he had to learn to dance. The Fosse film, Scheider's personal favorite, won him critical raves, an Oscar nod—and this tart tribute from TIME film critic Frank Rich: "Though Scheider is a wry, sensitive actor, he soon gets lost in the vulgar theatrics."

APPRECIATION

Jesse Helms, 1921-2008

HE WAS A CLASSIC POPULIST, PRESENTING HIS CONSERVATIVE agenda in plain terms that the average person could relate to. Of course, during his 30-year political career, Jesse Helms was considered controversial; he always thought his job was not to be popular but to do the right thing. He liked to quote his father: "The Lord does not require you to win, but he does require you to try." During his first decade in the Senate, Helms didn't win much. But after Ronald Reagan was elected, he was able to get a lot of bills signed into law with Reagan's help. Known as an unswerving conservative, he often worked across the aisle. In the 1990s, he and Senator Joe Biden collaborated on significant U.N. reform. And with an unlikely ally, U2's Bono, he secured some $200 million to fight AIDS in Africa.

—BY CHARLIE BLACK, *chief political strategist to Senator John McCain*

George Carlin, 1937-2008

LIKE HIS HERO LENNY BRUCE, GEORGE CARLIN SAW THE COMEDIAN as social commentator, rebel and truth teller, exposing hypocrisy and challenging conventional wisdom. He pointed out that America's "drug problem," for example, extended to middle-class suburbia, from office coffee freaks to housewives hooked on diet pills. Most famously, Carlin talked about the "seven words you can never say on television," foisting the verboten few on his audience with the glee of a classroom cutup and the scrupulousness of a social linguist. His intention was not just to shock; it was to question our irrational fear of language. —BY RICHARD ZOGLIN

Robert Rauschenberg, 1925-2008

IT MAY BE THE LEAST OF THE MANY THINGS THAT ROBERT RAUSCHENBERG will be remembered for. But in summing up the legacy of the artist, let's pause to remember that he won a 1983 Grammy Award for the cover of the Talking Heads album *Speaking in Tongues.* Something about that feels right. It's hard to think of a better match for Rauschenberg, a demiurge of creative disorder, than the band that said, "Stop making sense." What he passed on to everyone who came after him was an idea of art as a very freewheeling transaction with the world. True, many artists since have used the idea as permission to make lazy, slapdash work. So did he. But every time you see anyone doing anything that isn't supposed to be art—and calling it art—he is there.

Jamming his found objects together with abandon, Rauschenberg produced industrial-strength "combines," big pieces in which worlds collided with a bang. Maybe the most enduring idea he left us is that one great task of art is not so much to impose order but to make the most of chaos. —BY RICHARD LACAYO

Suharto, 1921-2008

HE HAD AN EERILY PRACTICED, BEAtific smile, a secular philosophy that tamped down religious extremism, and an anticommunist bent that made him a key cold war ally for the U.S. Yet army general Suharto was also a brutal dictator who purged hundreds of thousands of critics as Indonesia's ruler from 1967 to 1998. He was forced to step down in the wake of the Asian fiscal crisis, but the controversy over his reign continued. Indonesia's new government launched inquiries into the corruption. Suharto sued TIME after it published its own 1999 investigation into his ill-gotten gains. He won his lawsuit on appeal; TIME is challenging the decision. He spent his postrule years living in comfort and avoiding trial for his abuses.

Charlton Heston, 1923-2008

NOBODY WANTED TO SEE CHARLTON HESTON IN THE BUSINESS SUIT or polo shirt that other stars of the 1950s and '60s wore. The present was too puny a place to confine him. But put him in a toga or a military uniform from any millennium, or strip him to the waist to reveal that finely muscled torso, then let his tense, intense baritone voice articulate a noble notion, and you had Hollywood's ideal of Mensa beefcake. In the era of the movie epic, he was the iconic hero, adding to these films millions in revenue, plenty of muscle and 10 IQ points. The movie Heston was almost his own species: Epic Man.

Heston was unique among Hollywood stars. Of no other actor could you say, He was born to play Moses, Ben-Hur, El Cid,

Michelangelo. At the very moment Marlon Brando was freeing film-acting from good manners, Heston proved there was thrilling life in the endangered tradition of speaking well and looking great. And when he wasn't the movies' avatar of antique glory, he was our emissary to the future in *Planet of the Apes* and *The Omega Man.* Heston was the alpha and omega of movie manhood—our civilized ancestor, our elevated destiny.

In the 1960s Heston marched with Martin Luther King Jr., and after Robert Kennedy's death, he called for gun control. But like many young liberals, he aged into conservatism. In the 1980s he became a prime spokesman for right-wing causes and in 1998 the president of the National Rifle Association (NRA). At the 2000 NRA convention, he invoked his own Moses, hoisting a rifle above his head and proclaiming that presidential candidate Al Gore could remove the gun only by prying it "from my cold, dead hands."

Heston had a final great role to play. In 2002 he announced that he was suffering from Alzheimer's-like symptoms and, in a last burst of eloquence, declared, "I must reconcile courage and surrender in equal measure." Not even a movie hero can write a happy ending to his own life, but maybe in the enveloping vagueness, Heston had one. With him when he died was Lydia Clarke Heston, his wife of 64 years.

From start to finish, Heston was a grand, ornery anachronism, the sinewy symbol of a time when Hollywood took itself seriously, when heroes came from history books, not comic books. —BY RICHARD CORLISS

Arthur C. Clarke, 1917-2008

SCIENCE FICTION WRITER ARTHUR C. CLARKE'S LIFELONG FASCINATION with the myriad possibilities of space exploration helped ring in the space age. Lured as a boy by sci-fi magazines and his own homemade telescope, Clarke studied physics before turning to writing full time. Among the advances he foresaw in more than 100 works: space travel, geosynchronous communications satellites and computers.

His writing, most famously the futuristic novel *2001: A Space Odyssey,* often gave voice to the theme of humankind gaining enlightenment from contact with alien life. He believed E.T.s would send a sign, noting as recently as 2007, "We have no way of guessing when ... I hope sooner rather than later."

Isaac Hayes, 1942-2008

HE PACKED A LOT OF ACHIEVEMENT INTO HIS 65-YEAR LIFE: Isaac Hayes wrote hit songs, produced platinum albums, starred in movies and on television. But the biggest triumph for this self-described Black Moses had to be in 1972, when his theme for *Shaft*—a cunning mix of *wocka-wocka* percussion, a sassy chorus and Hayes' basso talk-singing— won an Academy Award for Best Original Song, making him the first African American to win a music Oscar.

Producing many of the Stax hits of the 1960s, Hayes dispensed with the pop craftsmanship of rival Motown Records and revved up the testosterone. His imposing frame, and a stare that managed to intimidate and seduce, made the songwriter a natural for performing, even in his unlikely role as Chef, the school cook who dished out age-less wisdom on the animated show *South Park*. He was the pulse of sexual liberation, the erotic sound of black power, the voice of our best bad thoughts. —BY RICHARD CORLISS

Yves Saint Laurent, 1936-2008

WIDELY CONSIDERED THE GREATEST FRENCH COUTURIER OF HIS GENER-ation, Yves Saint Laurent was also credited with democratizing fashion and empowering women with his strong, sexy silhouettes. He famously brought the vernacular of the street to high-fashion runways—with motorcycle jackets, peacoats and berets—and put women in men's clothing, specifically the tuxedo, or Le Smoking. Inspired by artists like Mondrian, Picasso and Matisse, he aimed to make women look beautiful and feel confident. He did both effortlessly. Born in Algeria, Saint Laurent went to work for Christian Dior in Paris, eventually tak-ing over the fashion house after Dior's death in 1957 and then starting his own label. At the celebration of his 40th anniversary as a designer, he told TIME, "I am amazed, even quite astounded, that I could have lasted so long in fashion, and that people still love me." —BY KATE BETTS

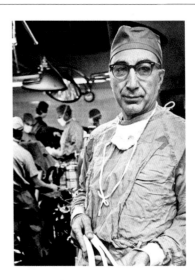

Michael DeBakey, 1908-2008

CONSIDERED BY MANY THE FATHER OF modern cardiac surgery, Michael DeBakey pioneered techniques and devices that revolutionized his field and still persist today. In 1932, while in medical school, DeBakey invented a pump that became a critical part of machines that later enabled open-heart surgery. He was one of the first to recognize the link between smoking and lung cancer, and he per-formed the first successful coronary bypass. He also provided medical advice to some of the most important leaders of the 20th century.

APPRECIATION

Heath Ledger, 1979-2008

EVEN WITH HIS BIG FACE AND CHISELED JAW, HEATH LEDGER WAS ONE OF those guys who blended in easily. In November 2005, waiting for me outside a pub, as he would've called it, he looked like any other scruffy twentysomething in Brooklyn, N.Y. He was a little bleary-eyed from being a new father but also a little wary of the press from being a heartthrob. We were meeting to discuss what would be his Oscar-nominated performance in *Brokeback Mountain*. We went to a local café; he didn't eat. Ledger was serious about—and not that impressed with—his work, trying to move from romantic lead to renegade. "I wanted to scrub it all away," he said then of early forays into stardom, "and start again, to see what my abilities are, if there are any." We'll never know the extent of them: on Jan. 22, 2008, Ledger, 28, was found dead in a Manhattan apartment, the victim of an accidental overdose of prescription drugs. —BY BELINDA LUSCOMBE

Reviewing the Australian actor's role as the Joker in the 2008 blockbuster Batman hit *The Dark Knight*, TIME film critic Richard Corliss wrote, "This Joker is simply one of the most twisted and mesmerizing creeps in movie history ... [Ledger] is magnificent ... he's the terrorist as improv artist. Evil is his tenor sax."

APPRECIATION

Jo Stafford, 1917-2008

SHE WAS AS FINE A MUSICAL ARTIST AS ANY in the 20th century, up there in a group that included Ella Fitzgerald, Judy Garland and Peggy Lee. Jo Stafford sang directly in the center of the note, and her sound was as clear as a Spanish town at noon. Stafford was also remarkable for the diversity of the material she tackled. She was one of the greatest ballad singers who ever lived, but she sang pop songs as well as folk music, country songs and novelty numbers. During World War II and the Korean War, Stafford toured extensively, performing for U.S. servicemen. She was shy and neither greatly beautiful nor a huge theatrical presence. Yet when she sang, servicemen overseas felt as if they were at home.

—BY JONATHAN SCHWARTZ, *whose self-titled radio program airs on New York's WNYC.*

Albert Hofmann, 1906-2008

IN SEARCH OF MEDICINAL USES FOR A WHEAT FUNGUS IN 1943, SWISS CHEMIST Albert Hofmann unwittingly became the first person to trip on lysergic acid diethylamide, the mind-altering drug better known as LSD. After being exposed to a small amount, Hofmann experienced what he called "a stream of fantastic pictures, extraordinary shapes with intense, kaleidoscopic play of colors." He hoped the powerful substance could be used to diagnose mental disorders and was dismayed by the international backlash generated by its recreational abuse in the 1960s, when the drug was adopted by the hippie movement and touted by such enthusiasts as Aldous Huxley, Timothy Leary, Ken Kesey and the Beatles as a mind-opening gateway to higher consciousness. Hofmann fought to correct that perception in his 1979 book, *LSD: My Problem Child.*

Bobby Fischer, 1943-2008

IT WAS BOBBY FISCHER'S ATTITUDE ON AND OFF THE CHESS BOARD THAT infused his play with unrivaled power. Before Fischer, no one was ready to fight to the death in every game. No one was willing to work around the clock to push chess to a new level. But Fischer was, and he became the detonator of an avalanche of new chess ideas, a revolutionary whose revolution is still in progress. By World War II, the once strong U.S. chess tradition had largely failed. So for an American player to reach world-championship level in the 1950s required an obsessive degree of personal dedication. Fischer's triumph over the Soviet chess machine, culminating in his 1972 victory over Boris Spassky in Reykjavíc, Iceland, demanded even more. He declined to defend his title in 1975, and by forfeit, it passed back into the embrace of the Soviets. According to all accounts, Fischer had descended into isolation and anger. Much has been written about his subsequent disappearance and apparent mental instability. Some are quick to put the blame on chess itself, which would be a foolish blunder. Pushing too hard in any endeavor brings great risks. —BY GARRY KASPAROV

Bernie Mac, 1957-2008

NOBODY WANTED TO GO ONSTAGE AFTER BERNIE MAC. YOU WERE ALWAYS thinking, Can I do these things to the same audience? Mac had this freedom, this edge—one minute he was saying funny material, then he was cutting you deep, and then he was saying something that made you think. There was a frenzy to it. If you went on after him, even if you were funny, they couldn't laugh anymore; it hurt. Bernie killed them. Each night you could bet he was going to jump off the page in a way that no one saw coming. He was never trying to edit himself. As a comedian, that's the freedom you're looking for onstage, to be as honest you can be and say something so relevant, you're either going to be shocked or you're going to laugh your butt off.

— BY CEDRIC THE ENTERTAINER, *as told to TIME.*
Cedric starred with Mac in the original Kings of Comedy tour.

Margaret Truman,
1924-2008

LIFE IN THE GLARE OF WHITE HOUSE cameras was no fun for Margaret Truman, the only child of Harry Truman, and her early attempt at a singing career was not much easier. (When a critic panned her "flat" voice, the President warned that if they met, the critic would need "a new nose.") Still, the witty, level-headed Margaret found her calling in 1980 when she published the best-selling *Murder in the White House,* the first of a series of successful mysteries set in the FBI, Supreme Court and other political hotspots.

Studs Terkel, 1912-2008

FOR MORE THAN A HALF-CENTURY, STUDS TERKEL HAD AN ONGOING conversation with America. This elfin-looking man, usually dressed in a red plaid shirt, ventured out into the unfamiliar with tape recorder in hand and spoke with people whom he liked to call the etceteras of the world. In his presence, they mattered. He knew they had something to say—about race, about class, about work, about hope, about community. About America.

Terkel didn't just arrive at someone's front door and say, "Tell me about yourself." He carried on a conversation. And he didn't let people off the hook. In *Division Street*, a 19-year-old man who had left the hills of Kentucky for Chicago talks about his fear of living too close to blacks. "It doesn't bother me," he says, "as long as they stay on their side of the street." To which Terkel asks, "Suppose they're on the same side of the street?" You can almost hear the young man consider this for a moment before laughing at himself. "I imagine we might be able to be pious and get along pretty good," he replies. That was Terkel. His effervescence brought out the best in virtually everyone he encountered. His books brought out the best in America. —BY SIMON ROBINSON, AUTHOR OF THE AWARD-WINNING *THERE ARE NO CHILDREN HERE*

Richard Widmark, 1914-2008

FOR OLDER MOVIE FANS, HIS VISAGE MAY always evoke the cackling, maniacal villain Tommy Udo pushing an old woman tied to a wheelchair down a staircase, in the 1947 film *Kiss of Death*. Widmark's riveting screen debut as a sociopath won him an Oscar nomination, but offscreen, the Hollywood legend played the true gentleman. Over his career, the chiseled, unconventionally handsome actor portrayed a vast array of characters in more than 60 films— from frontiersman Jim Bowie in *The Alamo* to the head of a psychiatric institution in *Cobweb* to the corruptible boxing promoter Harry Fabian, one of his most memorable roles, in Jules Dassin's *Night and the City*. In private life, Widmark was an environmentalist and longtime supporter of conservation efforts.

Jim McKay, 1921-2008

THE BROADCASTER TRAVELED SOME 4 MILLION MILES IN HIS 37 YEARS WITH ABC'S *Wide World of Sports*, "spanning the globe," as its slogan put it, to bring viewers "the thrill of victory and the agony of defeat." And wherever his travels took him—from the Olympics to barrel-jumping to demolition derby—he brought a reporter's eye, a poet's touch and a little boy's enthusiasm.

But McKay's finest hour was sports' darkest, when 11 Israeli athletes perished in a terrorist attack at the 1972 Munich Olympics. Reporting the story over 16 uncertain hours, McKay was calm, capable, compassionate—and thinking of the parents of Israeli weight-lifter David Berger, an American who had immigrated to Israel. "I knew," he said, "that I would be the one to tell them if their son was alive or dead." When that terrible moment came, McKay looked into the camera. "My father used to say our greatest hopes and our worst fears are seldom realized," he said softly. Then, "They're all gone." It was an exquisite blend of professionalism and humanity.

—BY BOB COSTAS

Tony Snow

Eddy Arnold, 89, guitarist and singer who mixed pop and traditional country-music styles with great success but never stopped referring to himself as the "Tennessee Plowboy."

Neil Aspinall, 66, called the Fifth Beatle by members of the band, who took a long and winding journey from devoted roadie and unofficial manager to chief of the Beatles' music empire, Apple Corps.

Madelyn Dunham, 86, grandmother and surrogate mother of Barack Obama who helped raise him in Hawaii and impressed upon him her ethic of hard work and fair play. She died on the eve of the day Obama was elected President.

Clay Felker, 82, legendary editor who founded *New York Magazine*, edited the *Village Voice*, worked for *Esquire*, TIME and LIFE, and helped foster the late-'60s creation of New Journalism.

Phil Hill, 81, race car driver who won Le Mans three times and in 1961 became the first (and still the only) American-born driver to win the Formula One championship.

Tony Hillerman, 83, novelist who portrayed the American Indians of the Southwest with accuracy, color and affection—in short, as fully rounded characters—in his numerous best-selling mysteries.

Hamilton Jordan, 63, chief of staff to President Jimmy Carter, one of the youngest to ascend to the post, who served as a key adviser on both domestic and international affairs.

Harvey Korman, 81, who showed his comic genius as a straight man opposite Carol Burnett's over-the-top characters, as a regular on her show for more than a decade.

Dick Martin, 86, the zany half of the duo that glued Americans to their TV sets with the rumbustious late-'60s comedy hit *Rowan & Martin's Laugh-In.*

Anthony Minghella, 54, critically acclaimed British director of *The English Patient*, *The Talented Mr. Ripley* and *Cold Mountain* (among many others) and screenwriter.

Oscar Peterson, 82, exquisite, sophisticated pianist—perhaps jazz's greatest—who took the keyboard to new peaks of hard-swinging, dizzying improvisation, which he called a "daredevil enterprise."

Sydney Pollack, 73, director (*Out of Africa, Tootsie, The Way We Were*),

Levi Stubbs, second from left

producer and character actor who worked often with Robert Redford and blended a commercial appeal with an offbeat intellectual style.

Tony Schwartz, 84, who created the famed "Daisy" ad for the 1964 presidential campaign, and also did less celebrated work on campaigns for fire safety and AIDS awareness and to reduce cigarette smoking.

Paul Scofield, 86, British actor best recalled for his Oscar-winning performance as Sir Thomas More in the 1966 film version of *A Man for All Seasons* but who preferred stage to screen.

Tony Snow, 53, Bush Administration press secretary who earned credibility by his willingness to say the rarest words in Washington—"I don't know"—when he didn't have an answer.

Levi Stubbs, 72, singer and frontman for Motown's legendary Four Tops (*Baby I Need Your Loving, Reach Out, I Can't Help Myself*), whose golden, powerful and gut-wrenching voice was undeniably among the greatest of his time—and was matched by his heart and character.

John Templeton, 95, financial-industry legend and visionary who pioneered value investing beyond U.S. shores long before such global perspectives became commonplace.

Tasha Tudor, 92, beloved children's book illustrator whose work—like popular versions of Frances Hodgson Burnett's *The Secret Garden* and Clement C. Moore's *The Night Before Christmas*—was steeped in loopy sweetness.

Jerry Wexler, 91, music journalist turned producer who is credited with coining the term *rhythm and blues* and nurtured some of the biggest acts of the past half-century.